IRAQ
CAMPAIGN 2003
ROYAL NAVY AND ROYAL MARINES

C000070235

Published by Agenda Publishing
© Robert Fox 2003

All rights reserved. No part of this publication may be reproduced or transmitted
in any form or by any means, electronic or mechanical, including photocopying,
recording or by any information storage and retrieval systems without prior
permission in writing from the publishers. Multiple copying of the contents
of this publication without prior written approval is not permitted.

Photography by Royal Naval photographers:

CPOA(Phot) Dave Coombs
POA(Phot) Colin Burden
POA(Phot) Gary Davies
POA(Phot) Nathan Dua
POA(Phot) Jim Gibson RNR
POA(Phot) Tony Leather
POA(Phot) Tam McDonald
POA(Phot) Graham Meggitt
LA(Phot) Gaz Armes
LA(Phot) Sean Clee
LA(Phot) Nikki Harper
LA(Phot) Dave Husbands
LA(Phot) Angie Pearce
LA(Phot) Paul Punter
LA(Phot) Dave Walker

and other images supplied by the men and women of the Royal Naval Units

*Produced in co-operation with the Directorate Corporate Communications (Navy)
and in particular Lt Cdr Chris Mahony and CPOA(Phot) Wayne Humphreys*

*Photographs by Tom Stoddart (Title Page and Chapter 5) courtesy of
Independent Photographers' Group www.ipgphotographers.com*

First published in the United Kingdom in November 2003
by Agenda Publishing
36 Great Smith Street, London SW1P 3BU
www.agendapublishing.com
Designed by Tian Mullarkey

ISBN: Hardback 0-9545972-0-6
ISBN: Softback 0-9545972-1-4

Whilst every effort has been made to ensure the accuracy of the names and events
mentioned within this book, the Ministry of Defence, the publisher and the author
cannot accept liability for any omissions or inaccuracies in its pages. The views
expressed in the book are not necessarily those of the Ministry of Defence.

Printed and bound by Butler and Tanner Ltd.

foreword by

Admiral Sir Alan West KCB DSC ADC
First Sea Lord

Robert Fox's book tells the story of the men and women of the Royal Navy, Royal Marines and Royal Fleet Auxiliary who fought in the recent Gulf War alongside the British Army, Royal Air Force and coalition forces. This is not intended to be a definitive chronicle, but a collection of personal accounts given to the author in a series of interviews in the immediate aftermath of the conflict. I am sure that official and detailed histories will follow, but these personal accounts give an insight into the conduct of the war, and reveal the courage and determination of all those involved in the face of the most challenging and difficult circumstances.

I wanted to introduce this book as a means of conveying my deep gratitude to all those who took part in the Iraq Campaign, whether in the Gulf region itself or elsewhere supporting front line units. The contribution made by all arms of the Royal Navy, uniformed and civilian, was a vital element in the operational success of the combat operations. Of course the task is not over, with many remaining in Iraq working to secure a stable, safe and prosperous country for its people. Some, however, paid the ultimate price to achieve that goal. They will remain forever in our thoughts and prayers, and we as a Nation in their debt.

Admiral Sir Alan West KCB DSC ADC

Ministry of Defence
Old War Office, Room 231
Whitehall, London SW1A 2EU

1SL/PF/4/2/1

Admiral Sir Michael Boyce GCB OBE ADC
Chief of the Defence Staff

19 March 2003

Dear CDS,

Mindful that it is my primary responsibility as First Sea Lord to deliver and ensure the fighting effectiveness and efficiency of the Royal Navy, I write to confirm that the Service is in all respects ready for the demands that may be placed on it, and in particular on its people, over the next few days and weeks.

You will be aware that the contribution the Royal Navy is making to combat operations is significant. Our Special Boat Squadron is fully integrated within those forces designated for initial operations, and our two TLAM firing submarines are patrolling ready for the part that they will play. The Amphibious Task Group, with personnel of 3 Commando Brigade, elements of the Fleet Air Arm and Royal Air Force embarked, having arrived early in the Gulf are poised to contribute to operations ashore. Of the other surface units in the area of operations, frigates and destroyers are fully involved in Maritime Interdiction Operations, and our mine countermeasure vessels stand ready to clear the way, if needs be, to the ports of Southern Iraq. Our survey vessel HMS ROEBUCK has already shown its value in surveying in support of operational planning. The Royal Fleet Auxiliary has demonstrated, yet again, its vital contribution in forward sea basing, and in sustaining our forces both afloat and ashore.

While we cannot predict the course of events that may follow, I can assure you that the Royal Navy is ready for the task that lies ahead. As a Force Element Commander in a previous conflict, I can state with certainty that the Royal Navy today is better trained and equipped than it was on that occasion and equal to the challenges it now faces. In our people, their courage, commitment and morale, I have nothing but admiration and absolute confidence.

As ever

Alan

Copy to :

The Right Honourable Geoff Hoon MP
Secretary of State for Defence

Sir Kevin Tebbit KCB CMG
Permanent Under Secretary

Contents

THE NAVY GOES TO WAR IN IRAQ

CALL TO ACTION

The waters of the Northern Arabian Gulf can be a tricky and inhospitable place in the early months of the year. Temperatures plummet suddenly, the seas turn angry under the rage of the sand storms out of the desert, the Shemal.

It was in this season in February and March of 2003 that a task force of more than 33 ships and submarines of the Royal Navy and the Royal Fleet Auxiliary, with support vessels from the merchant service, assembled for the biggest allied amphibious operation since Suez in 1956. The ships and men and women of the service were part of Operation Telic, the British contribution to the American-led Operation Iraqi Freedom, which was to lead to the toppling of the regime of Saddam Hussein. One of the hardy perennials among the breed of world dictators, Saddam had ruled his country and people by fear and terror for just short of 25 years, at the cost of the lives of hundreds of thousands – possibly millions – of his fellow Iraqi countrymen.

HMS Ark Royal departs Portsmouth

The Navy and the Royal Marines were to contribute a substantial part of the British effort in the liberation of Iraq by land, sea and air, and, from under the sea, by Tomahawk missile launching submarines. Every operational branch of the Navy and the Marines would be involved in one form or another in operations, though the activities of some were – of necessity – clouded in secrecy.

The British Naval contingent was led by the three largest ships now serving in the Fleet: the carrier *HMS Ark Royal*, the helicopter carrier *HMS Ocean* and *RFA Argus* which became the principal allied hospital ship serving in the northern end of the Gulf. At the other end of the scale were six Mine Counter Measure Vessels (MCMVs), playing a vital role in clearing the treacherous channels to Iraq's two main ports, Umm Qasr and Basra. Frigates and destroyers gave gunfire support to operations ashore to seize Iraq's short coastline on the Al Faw peninsula.

Top: *HMS Ark Royal sails for contingency operations in the Northern Arabian Gulf*
Inset: *Operator Mechanic Scales is interviewed during a press conference onboard HMS Ark Royal*
Above: *Mk7 Sea King helicopters of 849 Naval Air Squadron*

Battle Physical Training for Delta Company 40 Commando Royal Marines

Virtually the entire strength of 3 Commando Brigade was sent into battle for the first time since the Falklands campaign. This time the script opened with a major difference in the story. When 40 and 42 Commando seized the Al Faw peninsula in an assault from the sea and by helicopter, they would be opposed – unlike the landings at San Carlos in May 1982. The choreography in 2003 was made hugely more complex by the scale of the operation and the requirements of working within the American-led coalition, which meant working closely with the Americans . In the narrow confines of the Northern Arabian Gulf (the NAG as it will always be known to those involved) the space was crowded for manoeuvre on the surface of the sea and the skies above. The British carriers and escorts were working with no fewer than five American giant carriers launching operations (including two in the Mediterranean). Hundreds of aircraft filled the sky. Helicopters had their ceilings restricted by the operations of Tomahawk Land Attack Missiles flying above them.

Top: *Royal Marines from D Company 40 Commando practise disembarkation drills during exercises en route to the Gulf*
Above: *Marines carrying a 50 calibre Browning heavy machine gun wait to board a Chinook helicopter from 18 Squadron Royal Air Force*

Clockwise from top: *RFA Fort Victoria, which provides the Royal Navy with stores, fuel and munitions, as well as a base for RN Merlin helicopters; RFA Argus, the Primary Casualty Receiving Ship (PCRS); HMS Brocklesby in the Arabian Gulf with a SWIMS (Shallow Water Influence Mine Sweeping) boat, which can be used from a Mother MCMV to remotely sweep mines; and RFA Sir Tristram in the Northern Arabian Gulf*

HMS Ocean departs Plymouth heading for the Gulf

Above: gunners practise gunnery drills using the ship's 20mm 'Gambo' close range weapon
Below: gun crews on alert during their Suez transit

Though the war broke out suddenly and almost prematurely in the early hours of 20 March, it had been brewing for a long time. It virtually started where the last one left off: the allied mission to liberate Kuwait from Saddam's occupying force in February 1991. (The presence and action of the Royal Navy had been required then, too, though on nothing like the scale on which they would be involved in 2003.) Ceasefire talks opened at Safwan in south-ern Iraq on 3 March 1991. The agreement made with the UN required Saddam to disarm, and to declare and destroy his chemical, biological and nuclear pro-grammes. He was bound to this by UN Security Council Resolution 687, which had the power of a treaty. For seven years, Saddam played cat and mouse with the UN arms inspectors who, even so, man-aged to make a lot of headway in discover-ing what weapons or materials existed, and making sure that quantities of weapons, missiles and the like, were destroyed. In 1998 Saddam expelled the inspectors completely, leading in December that year to the four-day punitive bombing mission known as Operation Desert Fox.

With the passing of UN Security Council Resolution 1441 by all 15 members of the Council in November 2002, Saddam reluctantly agreed to readmit the UN inspectors. The hide and seek game of disclosure and non-disclosure with the inspectors was resumed. In December the Baghdad regime produced thousands of pages of documents about its defence industry and weapons stocks which failed to explain what had happened to the materials the inspectors had identified in 1998. (Apparently these materials, including precursors for a range of bacteriological and chemical weaponry, had just disappeared.) By January it was clear that the governments of America and Britain believed that war could not be long delayed. On 10 January, *HMS Ark Royal* and a number of escorts sailed.

Detailed planning of land, air and sea operations for a possible campaign had begun in August 2002. Rear Admiral David Snelson, the UK Maritime Component Commander, already had personnel 'embedded' – to use the new buzz word – with staff at the US Fifth Fleet. The admiral says he knew the Navy would be called on to make a major contribution "particularly in amphibious power projection. So my first job was to get the hardware safely there."

Top: *a Chinook helicopter onboard HMS Ark Royal*
Middle: *HMS Chatham patrols close to an oil platform taken by coalition forces at the start of the campaign*
Below: *HMS Splendid completing her last ever operational voyage following her successful involvement in the Iraq campaign*
Opposite: *HMS Liverpool in the Northern Arabian Gulf*

Just before Christmas leave most of those serving with the task group and 3 Commando Brigade were told they would probably be going to Iraq. In January most of the ships sailed, allowing a little time for some hasty training at Cyprus and later in the Gulf region. But just getting there raised big security risks. There was always the threat from Al Qaeda and its allies using small speedboats packed with explosive on suicide missions against allied ships in confined waters such as the Straits of Gibraltar, the Suez Canal, the southern narrows of the Red Sea, the Straits of Hormuz and the northern coasts of the Gulf itself. The Type 22 frigate *HMS Cornwall* with two Lynx helicopters aboard was dispatched as a guardship off Gibraltar. The threat was real: a number of Al Qaeda cells had been discovered in Morocco.

By the beginning of March, most of the British components of the coalition force were ready for action: the troops in Kuwait, aircraft stationed across the Gulf and the naval units at sea – a total force of 46,000 service men and women. The main tasks, or lines of operation, of the Navy and Marines would be to escort the forces by air and sea to battle; to be the spearhead of a major amphibious assault on the Al Faw peninsula; to clear the surrounding waters of mines and explosives; and to launch Tomahawk Land Attack Missiles from submarines. The Royal Marines went to help secure the port of Umm Qasr, where

Top: *a Royal Navy Merlin from 814 Naval Air Squadron picks up stores from RFA Fort Victoria*
Above: *Royal Navy SWIMS boats*

Air Engineering Mechanic Gordon on a quad bike embarked for the contingency operations

RFA Sir Galahad delivered the first large consignment of food aid, and helped seize Iraq's second city of Basra. Although, predominantly, British forces were under American command, there were American forces, such as the 15 Marine Expeditionary Unit, under British command.

In securing the southern entry into Iraq, the Navy, the Marines and the RFA played a vital role – and this book is their story. They provided support and forces for the taking of Umm Qasr and Basra, and the launch pad for the lightning American drive to Baghdad, which US forces seized on 9 April.

By late summer most of the units that had endured weeks of hectic action in Iraq in the Gulf in the spring of 2003 were home. But that was not the end of the story. Other ships returned to Gulf waters, to support the allied forces still in Iraq and to maintain a watch on the continuing threat of terrorist attacks from the Indian Ocean and the long tropical coasts of east Africa in Operation Enduring Freedom and the war against terrorism.

Royal Marines from Delta Company 40 Commando practise disembarkation drills alongside their embedded US Marines Air and Naval Gunfire Liaison and Coordination Officers (ANGLICOs)

HMS Liverpool's Lynx departing HMS Ark Royal

INTO ENEMY WATERS

As the main task force led by the big ships *Ark Royal* and *Ocean* was leaving British shores, one of the Navy's smallest ships was moving into enemy waters and to within a few miles of Iraq's coast. The coastal survey vessel *HMS Roebuck*, 1,200 tonnes and 63.9 metres long, is also one of the Navy's oldest ships. One of the first ships called *Roebuck* fought the Spanish Armada in 1588, and the ship has a dozen major battle honours to her name.

Before Operation Telic, it had been decided that *Roebuck* was due for her pension, as the Navy no longer had much use for a survey ship of this size and class. So valuable was the vital hydrographic surveying carried out by the 52-strong company that the ship's decommissioning was postponed.

"It was during this period that permission was granted for the Survey Motor Boat (*Bachelor's Delight* – Callsign SIERRA ONE) to enter Iraqi Territorial Waters," tersely notes the *Roebuck*'s War Diary of the first incursion by a British naval vessel into Iraqi waters. In the hours of darkness and early dawn, the *Bachelor's Delight* with its crew of five surveyed the shipping lanes of the Khawr abd Allah leading to the port of Umm Qasr. The results of the survey were transmitted by satellite to the UK for distribution across the task group as it made its way south and through the Mediterranean. Individual charts and surveys were burnt onto CDs and then taken by boat to be delivered to the leading ships arriving in the NAG (Northern Arabian Gulf).

A Royal Navy Sea King helicopter flies past an upper deck sentry manning a General Purpose Machine Gun (GPMG)

The *Bachelor's Delight* would stay out working for up to ten hours at a time. For most of January and February the boat worked with the frigate *HMS Cumberland*, which acted as guardship. During February came the dramatic switch – *Roebuck* was 'chopped' to direct American command. "There was no announcement, secrecy had to be kept," says Lt Commander Andy Swain, *Roebuck*'s commander.

For much of his 24 years in the Navy, Andy Swain has found his life intertwined with that of *HMS Roebuck*. He joined as a direct entry Junior Seaman at the age of 17. He served two years in the veteran destroyer *HMS Glamorgan* (of Falklands fame) as Navigator's Yeoman. In 1987 he entered Dartmouth and was commissioned, and returned to *Roebuck*, where he had served before, this time as Operations Officer for two years.

Top: HMS Roebuck on the Az Zubayr river, off Umm Qasr
Inset: onboard one of Roebuck's craft, Bachelor's Delight. Survey Recorder Nigel West mans the bow
Above: Survey Recorder Rachael Allcock mans a GPMG as part of the ship's force protection team

RFA Orangeleaf on transit through the Arabian Sea

Above right: Royal Marines from Delta Company 40 Commando carry out weapons training onboard HMS Ark Royal en route to the Gulf

Above: Marines 'zero' a 50 calibre Browning heavy machine gun

"No-one knows how to employ a surveyor," he says with a broad grin, "so I decided to write our two tasking signals myself." Initially the ship was ordered to Gulf waters for surveying operations for three months, and to return to Britain to be decommissioned by the end of March. Sailing on 11 November, Armistice Day, into hurricane force winds in the eastern Atlantic, the ship's company soon had other things to occupy their minds. West of Cape Finisterre they found a capsized yacht, and managed to call in a Spanish rescue helicopter to pick up the lone crew member.

By this time the *Roebuck* team felt they were heading towards war. Two General Purpose Machine Guns had been mounted – and the passage across the Bay of Biscay afforded some much needed gunnery practice. Some of the gunners, led by Leading Seaman Mick Walter, had previously fired a GPMG in anger from the decks of *HMS Ardent* in the Falklands.

Above and top: weapons drills and final weapon checks

For the protection of the ship's company, there was an even more urgent requirement than gunnery – the construction of a 'citadel' against biological and chemical attack in the heart of the ship. The building of *Roebuck*'s citadel has acquired the status of a legend in the Navy. Reports that it was made out of baked bean cans cannot be confirmed – but almost everything else in the do-it-yourself line was used. Materials and a training team came aboard in Gibraltar. The shelter was to be made from two large Winterbourne (field Nuclear Biological and Chemical Warfare) tents. However, they proved too big, so their filtration units were stripped and built into a citadel built by a team from the ship headed by the chippy, Chief Astley. The sanctuary covered the bridge, the wardroom and the officers' cabins. The bridge was sealed with tape and special putty, and wooden bungs were fitted into the main drainage points. Five days' food was stored as a standby, and on 21 November the new protected area was tested for ten hours.

Top: *a Royal Navy fireman keeps an eye on the flight deck of RFA Fort Victoria while Merlin helicopters of 814 Naval Air Squadron operate from her deck in the Northern Arabian Gulf*
Above: *a Lynx Mk3 takes off from HMS Liverpool's flight deck*
Right: *Royal Navy helicopter maintainers from 814 Squadron take a break in the hangar on RFA Fort Victoria between sorties*

Above: loading a drill torpedo onto a Merlin helicopter of 814 Air Squadron embarked in RFA Fort Victoria
Left: sailors prepare the chaff launchers onboard RFA Fort Victoria
Below: onboard HMS Edinburgh. Sailors store ammunition for her 4.5 inch gun

Roebuck began serious survey work in the Gulf in mid December, breaking off for Christmas. ("Easily the low point of the deployment," remarks the log.) Commander Swain said morale shot up immediately as the work resumed in earnest afterwards. He was sometimes in daily consultation with British and American commanders, particularly the staff of the UK Maritime Component Commander, Rear Admiral David Snelson. "I made the point of briefing the ship's company as much as possible – telling them exactly what was going on, as far as I could. We were told to watch CNN for news of developments in the political situation." New communications equipment was installed to ensure quicker distribution of survey information to the task group.

Some of that information turned out quite a surprise. Andy Swain and his hydrographers had honed their skills in surveying the complex tidal waterway of the Thames estuary. The Khawr abd Allah (KAA) and the Shatt al Arab (SAA) leading to Basra proved to be of similar complexity. The big question was how close could the big ships of the Amphibious Task Group like *Ocean* and *Ark Royal* get to the Iraqi coast, and in particular the first objective of the Al Faw peninsula? It turned out that parts of the waterway were several metres deeper than had been suggested by most current charts, which were mostly based on surveys of at least 30 years ago. The new surveys meant that the destroyers and frigates designated for shore bombardment duties to support the attack on Al Faw could move several miles closer inshore towards their targets.

Many of the new surveys were delivered personally by *Roebuck*'s captain to the British and American commanders in the task force now assembling. One boat crossing to the *USS Valley Forge* in a mid February gale is remembered as particularly horrendous. There was a host of other hazards – natural and man-made – for *Bachelor's Delight* (a name the American radio operators could not get their tongues round). Always there was the threat of mines, and of the numerous wrecks from previous wars. And there was the problem of local traffic, weaving in and out of the coastal dhows, some coming as close as 200 metres.

Time and rules of engagement put on more pressure. At first *Roebuck* herself was ordered not to go into Iraqi waters – though *Bachelor's Delight* could. "We surveyed from shallow to deep; usually it is the other way round," says Command Swain. Information had to be got to the ships on shore bombardment duty and the Mine Counter Measure Vessels (MCMVs) well ahead of the start of the campaign. Most of the work was completed well ahead of schedule – involving hours of duty on *Roebuck*'s spacious bridge, judged by Lt Gary Manning as "the best bridge in the Navy" for its all-round vision.

Top: *Operator Mechanic Leigh Mears, from Huddersfield, fires a GPMG*
Above: *Operator Mechanic 'Stretch' Armstrong carries out drills on a GPMG*

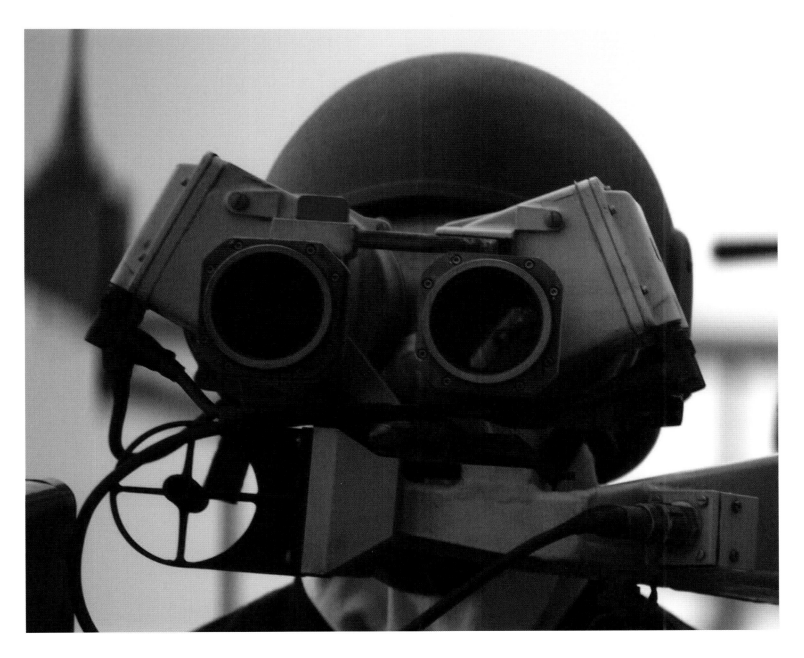

Top: *Scanning the horizon*
Above: *a Petty Officer loads a chaff rocket into its launcher*

Above: the remains of an Iraqi gunboat lie off the port of Umm Qasr
Below: upper deck sentries patrol around the decks of Royal Navy ships during the Suez Canal transit

Two weeks into the campaign and with much of her work done, *Roebuck* was given the honour of being one of the first Royal Navy ships into the port of Umm Qasr when she escorted the *RFA Sir Galahad* carrying hundreds of tons of humanitarian aid. Ashore the ship's company met old friends and colleagues, including the chaplain and hydrographer/met officer from *HMS Chatham*. But work wasn't quite over for the deployment. In two days *Bachelor's Delight* and her team completed a survey of the 12-mile stretch of waterway from Umm Qasr to Az Zubayr, now a forward base for the Royal Marine Brigade.

Leaving Umm Qasr for the open waters of the Gulf brought the last unpleasant surprise, and a stroke of real luck. Two large wrecks marked on either side of the main shipping lane proved to be nowhere near their marker buoys – one had shifted to within 70 yards of the main channel, and another was 150 yards off the main lane to the south. "We sat on one of them as *Sir Galahad* came out – those wrecks were real can openers."

Leading Airman Aircraft Handler 'Scouse' Griffiths practises his camera skills on the flight deck

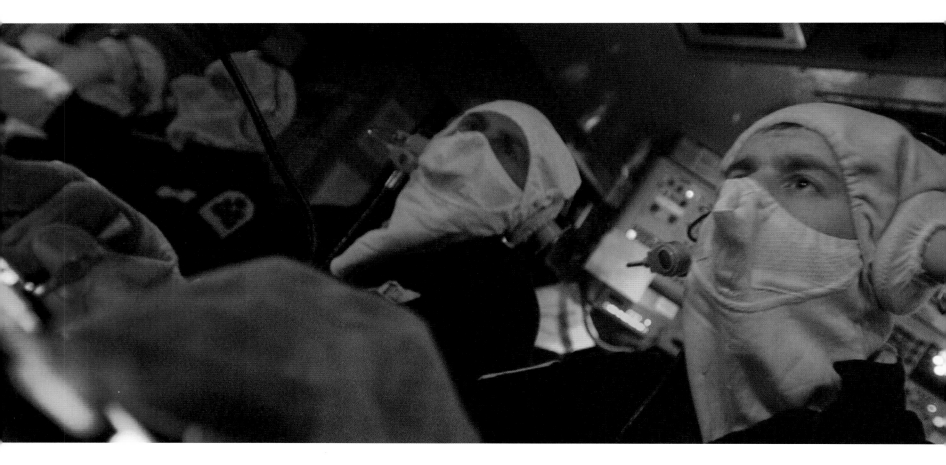

PLANS AND PLANNERS

While most of Britain was going on holiday in August 2002, the planners were preparing for the possibility of major operations in Iraq in the not too distant future. British and American naval commanders met in various Gulf locations on shore and at sea. Leading the British naval contingent was Rear Admiral David Snelson, boasting the some-what unwieldy title of UK Maritime Component Commander (UKMCC).

Not that the burdensome title would have worried him. He had recently commanded *Ark Royal* and had helped shape the Navy's thinking on amphibi-ous warfare. Renowned for his easy manner with all ranks above and below him, his natural courtesy conceals a mind of alarming clarity. David Snelson did as much as anyone to ensure the delivery of more than 46,000 British forces to the Gulf and the success of the opening phases of Operation Telic.

His role, he says, was that of "Supporting Commander, enabling the maritime contribution to a joint operation." His job was to help the Americans wherever possible and to supply crucial capabilities where they may have had gaps, principally in clearing mines. In this he saw the Navy as having four key roles:

✹ Escort duties for naval units from the Mediterranean to the Gulf, protecting coalition warships and merchant ships.

✹ The main amphibious effort to take and hold the Al Faw peninsula, and to prevent an ecological disaster from spilling and burning oil.

✹ The firing of Tomahawk cruise missiles from two Navy submarines in the Gulf.

✹ Mine Counter Measure Vessels in the Khawr Abd Allah and the Shatt al Arab to open Umm Qasr, then Az Zubayr and Basra for aid.

Above: *Rear Admiral David Snelson, the United Kingdom Maritime Component Commander (UKMCC)*
Right: *a sailor on the Type 42 destroyer HMS Edinburgh relaxes after a damage control exercise*

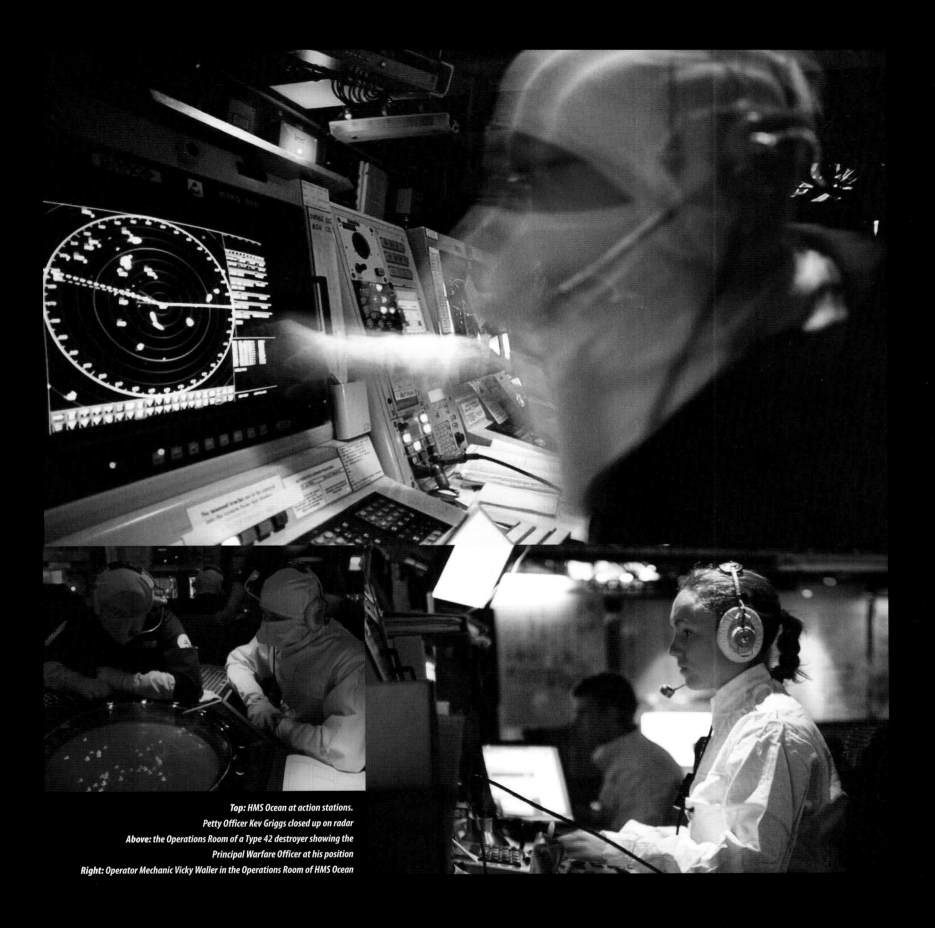

Top: HMS Ocean at action stations.
Petty Officer Kev Griggs closed up on radar
Above: the Operations Room of a Type 42 destroyer showing the
Principal Warfare Officer at his position
Right: Operator Mechanic Vicky Waller in the Operations Room of HMS Ocean

Admiral Snelson's team soon became 'embedded' with the staff of the US Fifth Fleet. He himself would shuttle between the Gulf region and the UK as the plans for the attack on Iraq were shaped.

The main effort for the Navy and its amphibious forces was to be the Al Faw peninsula. It guarded the approach up the sweep of the Khawr Abd Allah – always known as the KAA – into Umm Qasr, which was to be the main port for the delivery of aid. It had been hoped that the Al Faw coast would not be heavily occupied, otherwise the Iraqis could threaten the operations of the minehunters in the channel.

David Snelson knew he had slim resources compared with the Americans. The Americans were to mobilise five fleet carrier groups. The Navy had re-roled *HMS Ark Royal* to serve as a helicopter assault ship (LPH), with the dedicated LPH *HMS Ocean* also available. The old assault ships *Fearless* and *Intrepid*, veterans of the Falklands, had been decommissioned. At first it was hoped that only one commando, at enhanced battalion strength of about 1,000, would be needed to take and hold the Al Faw coast. By December it was clear that almost the entire strength of 3 Commando Brigade would be required. Intelligence indicated that the Iraqis were likely to move into the Al Faw and blow the oil terminals and pipes under the sea, causing pollution and disaster the length of the Gulf. The Royal Marines had to stop them.

The Commando Brigade under Brigadier Jim Dutton arrived in the Gulf with 30 days of supplies, including full scales of ammunition. Some 25 days' supplies were given to forward units of the 1st UK Armoured Division. Soon the minehunters were preparing to work with the Americans, working out how to fill the gap in American capability in disposing of ordnance under water.

Top: *a Sea King helicopter from 820 Naval Air Squadron carries out load lifting from the flight deck of HMS Ark Royal to other ships in the task group*
Above: *HMS Ocean's hangar crammed with aircraft of 845 and 847 Squadron*
Opposite: *Vertical Replenishment with 820's Mk6 Sea King*

Above: *onboard HMS Chatham, a Royal Marine from the Fleet Protection Group practises boarding operations*
Below left: *all officers and ratings in the task force had their respirators rechecked in the Mobile Nuclear Biological Chemical Defence Test Chamber*
Below right: *Air Marshal Brian Burridge, the United Kingdom National Contingent Commander, meets Royal Marines at Basra Palace*

Above: Lynx and Gazelle helicopters on the flight deck of HMS Ocean during a thunderstorm off Cyprus
Left: Maritime Planning Headquarters, Bahrain
Below: Lt Commander Ken Sprowles (left) and Commander Keith Hart (both RN Reservists) study charts in the United Kingdom
Maritime Component Commanders Headquarters, Bahrain

Once the battle was joined, David Snelson was in touch with his forward units, his American allies and the Joint HQ in the UK via radio, telephone, e-mail, internet websites and chat rooms on line. He was allowed access to the US net, and the coalition net COWAN (Coalition Wide Area Network). "It was different from anything before," he explains. "For the first time in my HQ, the use of UHF radio was minimal once operations began. I could talk via chat room within seconds of one of our submarines launching a missile."

Early in the operation came the setbacks. ("They usually do," says the Admiral). First the CH-46 American Sea Knight helicopter went down with eight personnel of the Commando Brigade's reconnaissance party aboard – five commandos, two soldiers and a sailor. "It was a really tragic setback," he says.

Some 24 hours later, two Sea King Mk7 helicopters of 849 squadron collided. "It really was a bad night," says the Admiral, but with a steady hand on the tiller he insisted the operations should continue.

Working closely with Admiral Snelson was Commodore Jamie Miller, Commander of the Amphibious Task Group (ATG) for Operation Telic – also known as 'the General'. (The tag comes from his time as Commander of *HMS Ark Royal*, and his insistence on attention to detail.) His passion for military history is legendary, so too is his ability to talk to any in his command without rank or rancour. He frequently presents his guests with a model lead soldier as a token of esteem.

Working from his operational headquarters in *HMS Ark Royal*, Commodore Miller describes his mission simply: "Our job was to unlock the door for the other forces." He spent the early months of 2003 drawing together his diverse – and, by British standards, large – amphibious force, with no fewer than 22 ships in the front line, 48 helicopters, and between 6,000 and 8,000 men and women under his command. Ships were commissioned, including merchantmen, roll-on roll-off ferries, and barges diverted from their usual trade.

Top: *aircrew onboard HMS Ark Royal show off their 'flying gas masks'*
Above: *two Sea Kings from 845 NAS flying low over southern Iraq*

Chinooks from 18 Squadron RAF test the
aircraft's heat-seeking missile counter-measures

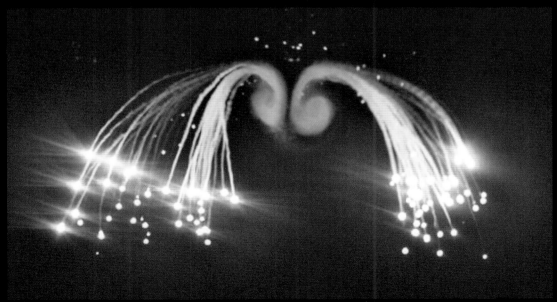

Above: *aircraft maintainers from 18 Squadron carry out an engine change on a Chinook*
Left: *a Royal Marine overseeing a Chinook lifting a vehicle into the Kuwaiti desert*

"We had to prepare for the worst, always look for the adder in the undergrowth," says the Commodore. The main task was "to get rid of the threat – rocket propelled grenades fired from the shore, the obstacles in the KAA and mines." One of the biggest problems was disposing of waste ('gash' in naval parlance) from the ships off the coasts of Kuwait. The gash barge assumed strategic significance and operated with an armed guard – any careless disposal of rubbish from the ships would disclose their presence and their plans.

Jamie Miller made it his business to draw together all those under his command to be a team. "It sounds old fashioned I know, but it was the principle of Nelson's band of brothers." A veteran of the Falklands, serving aboard *HMS Coventry* when she was sunk off Falkland Sound, he had learned the value of trusted colleagues. To help him, he recalled Chief Communications Yeoman Trevathon from *Coventry* days. "He was serving in Gibraltar, but came at an hour's notice."

The other arm of the team was commanded by Brigadier Jim Dutton, Commander of 3 Commando Brigade, which was about to undertake the most complex amphibious operation since the Falklands campaign, when he had been signals officer with 40 Commando.

He was concerned that the Iraqis might use the maximum fire power thay had, but knew the Marines would win once established on the ground.

However, this would be no orthodox landing. "We had no separate Amphibious Operations Area, and we were working within a coalition – unlike the Falklands." The Brigade came under command of the US 1st Marine Expeditionary Force. Lower down, the 15th US Marine Expeditionary Unit was placed under command of the Royal Marines.

The big difference from the Falklands experience was that, against the standard doctrine for British amphibious operations, the landing would be opposed. The Iraqis had forces in Al Faw. "We believed there was a good chance that chemical weapons would be used, and helicopters shot down. I never thought it would be a Palm Sunday procession as some predicted," says Brigadier Dutton.

The resistance was local and intense. Jim Dutton believes that the speed and violence of the assault caused the central command of Iraqi forces to break down. When the first large group of Iraqi troops surrendered to 40 Commando outside Al Faw, most of the officers had been shot – most by their own men.

Above: *Royal Marines on patrol in southern Iraq*
Below: *Queen's Dragoon Guards with Iraqi children*

Above: a 'pow-wow' between, from left to right, CO HMS Ark Royal Captain Alan Massey, CO HMS Ocean Captain Adrian Johns, Commander Amphibious Task Group Commodore Jamie Miller, and CO 40 Commando Lt Colonel Gordon Messenger

Above: a Sea King Mk4 from 845 NAS, HMS Ocean, carries out a final approach to the ship after ferrying men and supplies ashore

The biggest hazard initially was the weather. "We are supposed to have only five days in the whole of March when we can't fly in this part of the Gulf. By only the middle of March we had been unable to fly for seven." The US Navy Seals, the special forces demolition teams, had to go in by helicopter and on the night of 20 March they very nearly did not go in at all. In the crash of the CH-46 Sea Knight north of Kuwait, Jim Dutton lost a vital part of his Brigade Reconnaissance Team – and the Americans suspended flying operations. This underlines one of the important lessons of the campaign – the need for all-round support for expeditionary operations.

The Royal Marines benefitted from the back-up of Army artillery, the Challenger 2 tanks and, most important of all, the reconnaissance Scimitars of the Queen's Dragoon Guards, who earned themselves the title of 'Royal Marines Light Horse'. For the future, Jim Dutton says the British will have to take "a little bit of everything that you need."

Top: *Lt Colonel Simon Wolsey RA talks to his troops during Operation Telic*
Above: *Admiral Sir Jonathon Band, Commander-in-Chief Fleet, visits members of 3 Commando Brigade*

AL FAW
AND AFTER

"Oh well, here's another one," thought Sergeant Mark Donaghey of Bravo Company 40 Commando on receiving the news that his unit was headed for the Gulf. In the past two years he had been involved in operations in Afghanistan and Sierra Leone, so another order to move to war seemed a matter of routine.

With Bravo Company he would be in one of the first British units to go into action in the land war for Iraq. On the evening of 20 March, he and his team were lifted by helicopter out of their holding area in Kuwait into a murky night sky heavy with the remnants of a sandstorm still in the air. Less than an hour later they were landed at their target on the Al Faw peninsula, with its vital oil manifold station and pipelines leading out into the sea.

For the next three and a half weeks, 40 Commando would be involved in some of the heaviest action seen by British forces in the initial phases of the war, leading up to the capture and liberation of the port of Basra on 8 April. To their north, 42 Commando provided a screen, captured key points along the north of the Al Faw peninsula, and secured the advance on Umm Qasr.

A Royal Marine of 42 Commando takes up position beneath one of the many pictures of Saddam in Basra

On 30 March, most of 40 Commando, backed by Lima Company of 42 Commando, carried out Operation James – an all-day action involving tanks and attack helicopters on Al Khasib, on the stretch of fertile ground and date groves marking the approach to Basra from the south. It was one of the most complicated operations undertaken by a Royal Marine Commando in more than 50 years. From there the Marines moved into Basra, helping to liberate Saddam's summer palace on the shores of the Shatt al Arab waterway.

The action throughout was sporadic, but episodically intense – and very taxing physically. Transport and back-up were limited once on the ground and the men of Bravo Company had to make the approach to the forming-up position for Operation James by a 15 kilometre yomp carrying full kit, including Milan missiles and heavy machine gun ammunition.

During the opening phase of the assault on Al Faw, the two Commandos fought classic all-arms battles, with some help from armour and heavy fire support from British and American artillery on Bubiyan Island in Kuwaiti territory, plus the guns of the three British frigates and one Australian frigate offshore. More than 5,000 rounds of the Royal Marines' own mortars were fired, most covering 40 Commando operations.

Above and below: *Royal Marines of Delta Company 40 Commando disembark from HMS Ark Royal to take part in military operations on the Al Faw peninsula (photos taken through night vision goggles)*

This page: Royal Marines from Delta Company 40 Commando take a moment to reflect before disembarking to take part in operations ashore

Allies were involved, too. The Commando Brigade took the US 15 Marine Expeditionary Unit under command. US jets, A10 tank busters and AC130 Spectre gunships flew in support of the first assault. American MH 53 Sea Stallion helicopters landed the first men of 40 Commando onto the muddy wastes of the Al Faw peninsula.

It came at a cost. As the first helicopters took off from the Tactical Assembly Areas in the Kuwait sand, an American CH-46 Sea Knight helicopter crash-landed, killing, amongst others, eight men of 3 Commando Brigade's reconnaissance group. On 30 March, in the course of river patrolling north of Umm Qasr in the delta of the Shatt al Basra canal north of Az Zubayr, Marine Christopher Maddison was fatally wounded.

Just one year short of the tercentenary of their first great battle honour, Gibraltar 1704, the Royal Marines, under the brigade command of Brigadier Jim Dutton, accomplished one of the most remarkable feats of their history. They took and held virtually the entire coast of Iraq – the 60 mile loop of the Al Faw Peninsula – and unlocked the approaches to the ports of Umm Qasr and Basra.

But this was essentially a complex small unit campaign. And it is best illustrated by a few snapshot accounts of how just a handful of those units fared in the mud, dust and oil of southern Iraq in the spring of 2003 (see pages 53-71).

Top: Royal Marines from 40 Commando rehearse disembarkation drills on exercise in Kuwait

Above: a Marine from D Company 40 Commando shortly after landing on the Al Faw peninsula

Above: *a Chinook drops another load of ammunition to the Marines on the Al Faw peninsula*

Top: Brigade Reconnaissance Force (BRF) 'zero' their weapons

Middle: Royal Marines 'zero' their weapons on the Eduria ranges, Kuwait

Above: Marine Mark Murphy from Fire Support Troop, B Company
40 Commando, with a .50 Browning

Left: 29 Commando Royal Artillery fire upon Iraqi positions on the Al Faw

40 Commando B Company: the Al Faw attack

'H' Hour for the launch of the attack was to be at 1900 Zulu (GMT) on the night of 20 March. The day had been full of sand and alerts for attacks by Scud missiles, possibly carrying chemical warheads. The men of Bravo Company loaded themselves and their heavy Bergens (packs) into American MH-53 Sea Stallion helicopters. As they passed down the lines of their comrades to get to the machines, they shook hands.

Their objectives were the oil manifold station, and the oil pipeline links, both outside the town of Al Faw. Nearby was a military installation, potentially a barracks for up to 2,000 troops. There was speculation that the 51st Division was on the way south under the command of a veteran who had won back the Al Faw for Iraq in the Iran-Iraq war.

"We didn't land where we expected," says Marine Dave Schorah, "and the military installation wasn't what it seemed to be in the intelligence." But within minutes the company was engaged, 12 Iraqis were captured and two killed. With the Spectre gunship – a converted Hercules transport bristling with artillery – covering from above, the men of Bravo Company managed to get a fine view of the military base.

"The lads with the Milan were ordered to take out the buildings – which they did. We saw the Iraqis running away through the mud flats." Marine Botham saw an Iraqi coming towards him to surrender, "but he just turned away and ran off with the others and they carried on firing at us, but it was from quite a distance."

Meanwhile, Sergeant Mark Doneghy and his men had been moving onto the second objective, the pipeline link. He recalls: "A lot of people started coming towards us. We fired three Milan missiles at a truck and some artillery positions." Fire was called from the mortars, and later from ships offshore. An air strike destroyed an Iraqi observation tower. "It was really quite impressive," says Doneghy. "The area was quite populated, with people running in and out of the date palms – we were helped to clear the groves by Delta Company."

Above: Marines from 3 Commando Brigade march into the US site in Camp Commando for the visit of General M. W. Hagee US Marines
Below: members of the Assault Engineers troop take members of 42 Commando through mine training, led by Colour Sgt Kev Morgan in Camp Gibraltar, Kuwait

Sgt Simon Hicklin 42 Commando cloaked in the white ensign

Above: *Lt Col Dick Watts RM briefs Brigade staff officers*
Left: *a Royal Marine Commando guards the port of Az Zubayr*
Below: *the CO of 42 Commando, Lt Col Buster Howes RM, briefs Brigade staff officers*

After 24 hours the local leadership asked to talk. "The locals came out and asked if they could bury their dead," says Doneghy. "One of them spoke good English." The Royal Marines had found, among the dead, bodies of Iranians from the bitter fighting along the Al Faw peninsula in the Iran-Iraq war of 1980-88. "It was a strange, muddy place, and it was odd that those muddy little pipelines turned out to be so important."

The first night of action had brought its share of frustrations for 40 Commando – though the outcome was ultimately successful. It had been planned that 'C' Squadron of the Queen's Dragoon Guards (QDG) would be landed with its three troops of Scimitar reconnaissance vehicles (which resemble light tanks) by the giant American hovercraft known as LCACs. At the last moment, it was decided that the landing site was too heavily mined, particularly with the virtually undetectable anti-personnel mines.

Instead, the landing of the Dragoons in Operation Houghton had to be postponed and then shifted to further up the estuary towards Umm Qasr. The QDG under Major Henry Sugden were to become hugely popular with the men of 40 Commando and would later play a decisive role in the advance to Al Khasib and to Basra. They came to be known as the "Royal Marines Light Horse" and were awarded the 3 Commando Brigade Flash at the end of the campaign.

40 Commando Alpha Company: clearing Al Faw town

As Bravo Company was rounding up prisoners, the men of Alpha Company were completing a busy series of actions after their landing by helicopter to the south of the main objective, and the small town of Al Faw itself. Marines Lester, MacDonald and Gunne remember the roads round the little town being crowded with thousands of people. Their orders were to clear the town overnight, and to set up roadblocks the following morning. "There were masses of people just going about their business," recalls Steve Lester. During the day eight Iraqis caught the men of 1 Troop in an ambush – though there were no casualties.

Towards evening, Captain Matthew Williams, commanding 2 Troop, received a warning to seize a building believed to be the Baath Party headquarters. The Company Commander, Major Justin Holt, prepared to attack the building with an 'H' Hour of 1800 local. The operation was to be an assault by three eight-man fighting sections. No artillery was to be used, for fear of hitting the hospital nearby. The warren of rooms inside was to be cleared one by one.

Grenades were thrown and shoulder-held LAW rockets and Minimi machine guns fired as the attack went in towards dusk. The Baath officers seemed to have dumped their uniforms and fled. The Marines moved swiftly through, executing their drill: opening a door, throwing a grenade and then spraying the room with machine gun fire.

Top: 539 Assault Squadron RM patrols waters off the Al Faw peninsula
Above: Royal Marine boats from 539 Assault Squadron sit outside the presidential palace in Basra shortly after it was secured

This page: members of Lima Company 42 Commando carry out river operations outside Basra Palace, checking fishermen and other boats on the Shatt al Arab

This page: Royal Marines from 40 Commando

Then came the last of the rooms, at the end of a long corridor. Steve Lester threw in the grenade and after a short pause, Marine Iain Macdonald stepped forward with his machine gun. Suddenly the room erupted into flame.

"I saw the fireball come straight towards me. My face seemed to squash in and I knew I was on fire." Rushing from the building he became a human torch, all captured on the unit video, and later shown on network television. The grenade had ignited a gas cylinder and the mixture of propane burned all the atmosphere in the room. Iain Macdonald was by now more than 25% burned, on his arms, legs and the back of his neck.

"I couldn't find a spot to roll around on the ground, but it only took a couple of seconds for them to put me out." Captain Williams feared the worst: "At first I thought I had lost the whole section." At the company base in the local fire station, the Medical Assistant Nick Guljaardt doused the Marine with water, gave him morphine and cut his clothes off. Within a day he was cleared for flying back to the UK where he later made a full recovery. "By then I was mega spun out," says Iain Macdonald.

42 Commando

Things had not gone well from the start for Corporal David Beresford of 2 Section 5 Troop Lima Company 42 Commando. He had had a bruising time during range practice in Northern Kuwait when shells had landed close by.

On the night of 20 March he and 42 Commando were to be dropped into the Al Faw peninsula by American helicopters to put in a block to the north of 40 Commando's area of operations round the manifold and pipeline stations. The Commando was then to clear north, beyond Umm Qasr, towards Umm Khayyal, having taken over from the US Marines.

The mission had been under way for half an hour when it was dramatically halted. A twin rotor American CH-46 Sea Knight helicopter – outward bound with UK and US servicemen of the Brigade Reconnaissance Team onboard – hit the desert. Conditions had worsened steadily, and that evening helicopter pilots said it was hard to separate the muddy terrain from the sky and the air was full of sand and dust. Many had to fly on instruments until they were over Iraqi territory.

The Royal Marines of 42 Commando saw the helicopter erupt in a ball of fire. Immediately flying operations stopped. The Marines then lay down in sleeping bags – only to be annoyed by the television reporters circling at the scene. More worrying was the decision to suspend all helicopter operations that night, which meant that 42 Commando had no transport from CH-46 helicopters, the allocated MH-53 Sea Stallions, and Cobra gunships.

Above and top: Marines on the ranges in Kuwait prior to the invasion of southern Iraq

Sergeant Matthew Wildgoose, commanding the Fire Support Group of M Company, wondered if his men would be able to launch into Iraq that night at all. "Then the RAF turned up with some helicopters. I never thought I'd hear myself say it of the RAF but I could have kissed their backsides."

Despite the delays, the RAF teams got 42 Commando into the blocking position at the neck of the Al Faw peninsula where they were directed towards their objectives – all named after daughters of officers and men in the commando: Zara, Olivia and Emily.

The Marines were heavily laden with Bergens and ammunition – so heavily laden, in one case, that a Marine snapped his ankle as he leapt from the helicopter.

The Queen's Dragoon Guards earned the nickname 'Royal Marines Light Horse' during the campaign thanks to their decisive role in the advance to Al Khasib and Basra. They were also awarded the Commando Brigade Flash (see page 55). ***Above***: QDG troops man up their Scimitar CVRT (Combat Vehicle Reconnaissance Tracked)
Below: members of the Plymouth Argyle away supporters' club on manoeuvres in the Gulf

Royal Marine all-terrain vehicle BV206 operating inside Iraq on the Al Faw peninsula

Above: *a Marine fires a 94mm anti-tank weapon*
Below: *Marines maintain a sense of humour whilst pushing through southern Iraq*

For the big man David Beresford, the experience of landing was surreal. "Al Faw was a real hole – a moonscape of mud flats. We had seen all the int [intelligence] photographs but they didn't give the picture. It was mud, like the Somme in the First World War, the sort of mud you sink into to your knees, and get covered with stinking oil. There were still the remains of the fighting in the Iran-Iraq war."

The close combat teams of the Commando had a lively time as the night drew into dawn. The biggest threat appeared to be from artillery fire from D30 guns hidden among the date palms. Several taxis in bright colours, white and red, appeared on the roads and then disappeared. The Marines thought they were being 'dicked', in Northern Ireland parlance – in other words, the drivers and passengers were spotting for the Iraqi artillery.

This page: 42 Commando take charge of their area in southern Iraq

Umm Qasr and Al Khayyal: 42 Commando

After four days in the blocking positions on the Al Faw peninsula, 42 Commando moved north to Umm Qasr, the main port for the reception of aid, and the town of Umm Khayyal. Here the Marines received good intelligence about the presence of a Baath Party headquarters. They knew the pattern of fighting was changing. Fewer Iraqi troops were appearing, and black uniformed 'Fedayeen' and Baath Party militias were carrying out most of the shooting.

Captain George Bennett of 3 Troop J Company 42 Commando joined the hunt for the party building. "The map we had was wrong," he says, but he knew he had to find a two-storey house where it was thought the Baath party kept an armoury.

Moving at night, the Marines came under fire from a rooftop. The troop replied by calling in mortar fire. A hole was blown in the wall of the house, and children ran out. Men and women

Top: *a Marine stands guard at the temporary HQ of 3 Commando Brigade in the Iraqi town of Umm Qasr*
Above: *42 Commando patrol Umm Qasr a few hours after leaving Al Faw*

alike were weeping and two men
inside were bleeding profusely.
Soon the Marines came on stacks of
weapons. Lt Jones of 4 Troop called for
back-up. On the way (and this still in
the dead of night), about 20 Iraqis
mobbed Captain Bennett's troop, and
as they did so a machine-gun opened
up from a roof opposite. "The Iraqis
didn't seem to mind," says Bennett,
"but we took cover in the doorways
and then moved on.

"We took a wrong turn and ended up
on the wrong side of 4 Troop's attack.
We were nearly killed by our own
side. But we got some very good information that night – which was really
useful for the attack on Basra. It made
us all feel very James Bondy. But the
day before – and I'll never forget this –
it was horrendous. The heaviest rain
I've ever seen."

Royal Marines from 40 Commando take up positions in buildings on the Al Faw peninsula

A Royal Marine from 3 Commando Brigade sits patiently in the back of a Land Rover passing through the suburbs of the recently secured town of Abu al Khasib, southern Iraq. An Iraqi T55 tank burns in the background

30 March: the busiest day – Abu al Khasib and the approach to Basra, 40 Commando, 42 Commando and C Squadron the Queen's Dragoon Guards (QDG)

Throughout the last week of March, 40 Commando secured the position on the Al Faw peninsula. On the 24th, an Iraqi Armoured Battalion of about 50 T-55 tanks appeared to be pushing out of Basra to counter-attack the Marines on the peninsula. In the battles involving combat aviation and the light 105mm guns of 29 Commando Regiment RA, at least 20 Iraqi tanks and armoured carriers were destroyed.

By the end of the week 40 Commando, with support from the Brigade, and from Lima Company 42 Commando and C Squadron of the QDG, prepared to move on the township of Abu al Khasib which would open the southern route into Basra itself. The town was flanked by date palm groves, concealing inlets where smugglers found secure harbours. It was known to be occupied by Baath Party militia, Fedayeen and possibly large formations of Iraqi regular armoured troops.

Operation James was the setting of a 19-hour battle on the streets and in the date palms. The main objectives were three vital bridges codenamed Sennen, Dalmatian and Sheep's Tor. By now the Marines had the support of C Squadron of the Royal Scots Dragoon Guards with their mighty Challenger 2 main battle tanks, the most effective tank in the Iraqi campaign.

For Sergeant Mark Doneghy, Marines Botham, Schorah and Murphy, the beginnings of Operation James were not auspicious. "We received orders at 1700 hours and were told to be on the line of departure by 0200," they recall. Almost no transport was available, save a few quad bikes and a broken Iraqi truck or two. That meant a 15 kilometre yomp in the dark across to the start position south of Al Khasib. "We were told to clear enemy within bounds, and our objective was the bridge codenamed Dalmatian" Each company was involved in the attack. "It was terrible, cold and muddy all the way."

42 Commando 'J' Company on the morning they entered Saddam's palace

Above: Royal Marines inspect a weapons haul recovered from a patrol in Umm Qasr in southern Iraq
Below: members of Lima Company display a cache of arms found and recovered in the palace of Saddam

Marine Mark Murphy remembers moving up route Goldfinger for the attack. (All their objectives had James Bond names – Brosnan and Connery were to feature heavily in their orders.) With an hour to spare, the Marines rested and chatted in the dank night air. Mark Murphy remembers discussing cricket – though he says he does not play and is not particularly interested. They had not slept for most of the previous day, and they would not for the day to come.

The battle was a rolling guerrilla fight. The combat teams advanced in the standard arrowhead order, and they had little cover. The mortars fired some smoke under the fire control of Corporal Nigel Roberts – as the artillery could not drop smoke rounds with the necessary accuracy.

In broad daylight the Marines took bridge Dalmatian. A company engaged a building full of Fedayeen, but most fled as the Marines advanced and took cover in the date palms, occasionally firing back with rocket propelled grenades and AK-47 rifles. "We collected a lot of weapons, but most of the Iraqis went home or gave up." By last light, Murphy's section and Bravo Company had reached their objective – "the only one to do so in time," says Murphy proudly. As they did so, they could see men of 'A' Company still heavily engaged at objective Collie. "We could see several enemy on the bridge and there was firing from across the river," recalls Murphy. "We could see the rounds splashing over, around the road and in the water."

The men of 'A' Company linked up with a troop of Challenger 2 Tanks of the RSDG. Marine Russell Cook felt "it was just like a Vietnam movie" as his troop followed one of the tanks up the main axis of attack. "I could see the mortar strikes as the Fedayeen fired at us." On the road the marines came across a white pick-up which had been targeting them. Aboard were a full colonel and his bodyguards (one was shot as he escaped). A stash of arms and bundles of money were found.

It was the heaviest day, too, for C Squadron the Queen's Dragoon Guards, now under the command of CO 40 Commando, Lt Col Gordon Messenger. Major Henry Sugden deployed the squadron as an established screen of three troops south-east and west of Al Khasib.

By the late afternoon, 2 Troop and the Brigade Recce Force had secured Sennen bridge on the eastern exit of the town. They then helped to take Sheep's Tor quickly, but soon after came under heavy fire from what appeared to be a Baath headquarters. "There was quite a bit of fire around the bridge by now and the troop came under RPG attack at 50 metres," says Major Sugden. The first Scimitar pulled back, but fell into a ditch and threw a track.

Under heavy fire, the crew got out and set about repairing the track, with the second Scimitar firing in support. During the repair, Corporal 'Vidal' Armstrong takes a break to swig a can of 7 Up. "I'm just bloody thirsty," he says to the astonished Marines. A few minutes later Lt Simon Farebrother and the troop pull clear and finally secure the bridge. "There were a lot of Fedayeen in black pyjamas running around and we were concerned they would fire on women and children," says Major Sugden.

Top: *a local Iraqi thanks a member of 40 Commando on the Al Faw peninsula*
Above: *42 Commando, on patrol in the area of Umm Qasr, with local children*

Above: Royal Marines from 3 Commando Brigade distribute their remaining rations to local Iraqi civilians before returning to the UK the following day. The Marines insisted the rations were handed out and not just destroyed as they normally are if not used

Below: a Marine from 3 Commando Brigade makes a new friend

To the west the troop supporting Alpha Company had an equally hairy time: for most of the day they were out in open ground. As the firing built up, a rocket propelled grenade scored a direct hit on the Dragoons' Spartan support vehicle. The crew piled out, but seeing their vehicle had not caught fire, piled back in. Grabbing a mortar and heavy machine gun, they started firing back. "What are you doing? We're supposed to be doing that," shouts a Marine. Moments later, Corporal Danny Glover fires a mortar which scores a direct hit on a Fedayeen position – and the Marines cheer.

None of the Marines or Dragoons was killed or seriously injured in the 20 hours of continuous action. "We were just living on adrenalin, and were completely exhausted by the end," says Sergeant Doneghy. Elsewhere the news was not so good. Major Steve Ballard of the UK Landing Force Command Support Group collapsed and died without warning from natural causes. In difficult action during river clearance by 539 Assault Squadron Marine Chris Maddison was injured and later died of his wounds.

Above: 539 Assault Squadron Royal Marines
Below: Iraqi children wave to passing Marines

Basra and after

At the end of March, 42 Commando cleared to the north of Umm Qasr and Umm Khayyal. On 27 March they launched a full company attack against Fedayeen positions to the north.

By the end of that week men of Lima Company moved with 40 Commando to the southern part of Basra, the second city of Iraq. With Kilo Company they cleared the date palms groves outside the summer palace. "Fire was sporadic and continuous but resistance wasn't very strong," they remember. Waiting for 24 hours outside the palace, a patrol discovered Margaret, a British resident married to an Iraqi some 30 years ago. "What took you so long?" she says. "The soldiers left here the day before yesterday."

For Captain George Bennett, the two days he had resting in the palace grounds on the edge of Basra allowed a sense of achievement. "We had done what we set out to do, and none of my team had been hurt." Low points there were, too – like the weeks to come sitting out in the Rumailyah oil fields (voted unanimously the dullest part of the deployment by all the Marines). And the lowest point? "When the helicopter went down at the landing site on the first night. I had a combat engineer beside me. I had to tell him that his brother had died in the crash."

Royal Marines from 539 Assault Squadron rest after action on the Khawr Az Zubayr waterway, in the marshes of southern Iraq

UNDER A SMOKE-FILLED SKY

by Tom Stoddart

"I had to go. A spirit in my feet said 'Go', and I went." So said Mathew Brady when asked why he had gone off to photograph the carnage of the American Civil War. Nothing much has changed in the last 142 years, except that, today, literally hundreds of photographers and TV cameramen are drawn to every conflict.

During Operation Iraqi Freedom I was the only photographer 'embedded' by the MOD with 539 Assault Squadron Royal Marines. The Marines' mission was to dominate the Khawr Az Zubayr waterways and marshes around southern Iraq's Al Faw peninsula. My assignment was to capture an intimate, very personal, photo-essay of the unit as they went about their business.

The photographs reproduced here graphically illustrate the range of emotions and feelings which flood through a small unit when a comrade is lost. Afterwards, 539's commanding officer Lt Colonel Nick Anthony said to me: "War is a disgusting business at every level. Anyone who says it's heroic hasn't been here or seen it."

Lt Colonel Nick Anthony, Commanding Officer of 539 Assault Squadron Royal Marines, prepares to address his men

Royal Marine Kevin Jones from 9 Assault Squadron is rescued after being wounded in action on a landing craft in the Khawr Az Zubayr waterway

Wounded Marine Kevin Jones is treated by a comrade and BBC cameraman, Steve Gray, who stopped filming to help

Exhausted Royal Marines after a night in action, being told of the death of a comrade

Iraqi woman and child collect clean water from British troops on the outskirts of Basra

T IS FOR TLAM AND TOMAHAWK

Christmas appeared to be put on hold for the company of the nuclear powered submarine *HMS Turbulent*. She had just completed an epic voyage across the south Pacific and was headed north for the Gulf and reunion with families when the signal was given to return thousands of miles to Singapore.

Planes had to be unbooked and booked again for the unexpected reunion in Singapore. The festivities went ahead. But everyone knew something was up – that the submarine and her crew had some serious business to transact before returning to home port in Devonport in the summer.

HMS Turbulent is a Trafalgar class nuclear powered submarine. The PWR1 reactor allows her to travel huge distances underwater – and, according to the specification, will only need refuelling twice in the boat's entire lifetime. With *HMS Splendid*, she is one of a number of submarines in the fleet fully equipped for firing Tomahawk land attack missiles, a fact of crucial significance in the emerging drama in the Gulf.

A Tomahawk cruise missile is fired from HMS Splendid (photo taken through the boat's periscope)

The Tomahawk cruise missile (technically a Tactical Land Attack Missile) can fly hundreds of miles over land and sea and hit a target within two or three feet, a metre at most. In the attacks on Baghdad in 1991, British journalists claim to have seen one winging down the main boulevards of Baghdad and executing a right hand turn at a crossroads before homing on the target. Such a tale may be apocryphal, but what is beyond dispute is the power and precision which the weapons give to naval operations, particularly when a deep land strike is required.

The Tomahawk was introduced to the Navy from the United States in the late 1990s and was first fired in anger from the Adriatic by *HMS Splendid* during the Kosovo conflict of 1990. Boats (the Navy always refers to submarines as boats, not ships) armed with Tomahawks were part of coalition forces for the Afghanistan campaign in Operation Enduring Freedom in 2001. More than 1,000 cruise missiles were fired from American planes and warships onto Iraq in 2003. A much smaller number were fired from the British boats – but these proved highly significant.

Top: *HMS Splendid*

Above: *crew on board HMS Splendid watching television in their cramped living quarters*

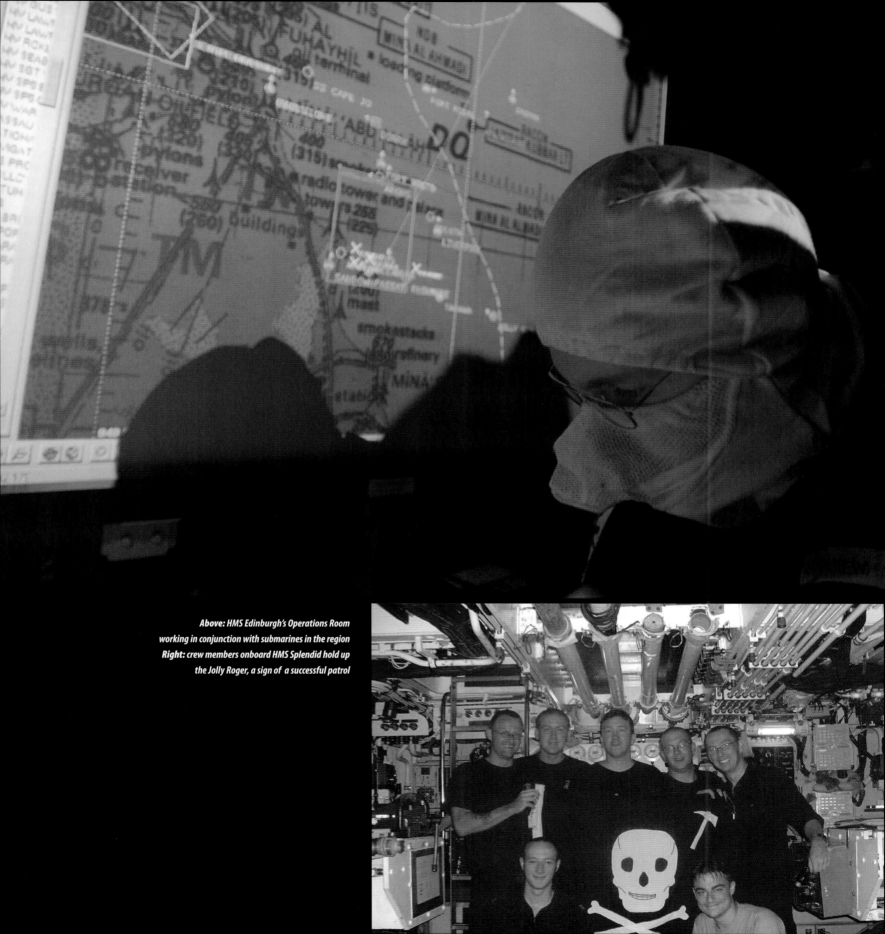

Above: HMS Edinburgh's Operations Room working in conjunction with submarines in the region
Right: crew members onboard HMS Splendid hold up the Jolly Roger, a sign of a successful patrol

HMS *Splendid* sailed from the UK and made passage through the Suez canal in early February, escorted by *HMS Chatham*. Once in the Gulf, she was victualled and loaded. In the space of a few days she would need to go in for a reload twice, and *Turbulent* was restocked with missiles once. Locations and timings of reloading were matters of high operational security and were not publicised until months afterwards.

Deep in the forward compartment of *HMS Turbulent*, the colour scheme is functional Navy black and a sickly light green. This is where the Tomahawks are prepared and loaded. Once prepared by the crews, they are sealed in their tubes. When it comes to the moment of firing there is little more than a dull thud and a whoosh.

Top: *looking into Splendid's Control Room*

Above: *HMS Splendid*

HMS Splendid completing her last ever operational voyage following her successful participation in the Iraq campaign

An officer and a weapons party look after the projectiles in the cradles day in day out. This was the domain of Petty Officer Darrell Heald. At 37, 'Daz' is a highly experienced weapons hand. "They functioned perfectly," he says of the missiles fired from the *Turbulent*'s tubes, the first fired from British boats in the Gulf. Five tubes would be prepared for action at two hours' notice. "We had been training for this for four whole months – you could say the atmosphere was highly charged!"

With just minutes to go, the Weapons Officer would check the settings and his assistants and deputies the seals on the tubes. From the Operations Room the signal was given for firing by a click of a computer mouse. The targets were hundreds of miles away, most in the Baghdad area. Four of the missiles would be fired in 45 minutes, and it took the weapons team 12 minutes to reload the tubes and carry out the checks. This impressed the Americans so much that they sent experts to watch Daz and his mates at work.

During the firing programme the weapons team in Turbulent were on call for 36 hours. In the lull between salvos, Daz managed to get his head down on a mattress in one of the missile's store racks.

Top: Commodore Miller, Captain Massey and Colonel Cox RM hold a press conference
Above: a news team interviews Commodore Miller

Top: Rear Admiral David Snelson, the United Kingdom Maritime Component Commander, is interviewed by Brian Barron of the BBC
Above: international press onboard HMS Ark Royal

As the first firings were due the Control Room suddenly became crowded. The Weapons Officers practised countdowns through their headphones. One of the officers witnessed through the periscope the moment of launch: "Bright lights under the surface of the water, then a ring of fire as the rockets set light to the surface."

"Nobody on board was gung-ho for war – and some hoped it wouldn't happen," says Lt Commander Richard Smallwood, the Executive Officer (XO). "But it was a bit of a double-edged sword: it was our ticket home." Most of the target information was held on board, relayed by satellite. One of the biggest puzzles was to 'deconflict' flight paths for the Tomahawks on air routes crowded with helicopters and strike planes going in for the attack. Shooting times and heights had to be logged and relayed across the task group by the flight controller teams in all the carriers.

The great skill of the *Turbulent* and *Splendid* teams was in 'spinning up' their missiles in record time. 'Spinning' in this sense means preparing the gyros and guidance systems housed in the nose of the missiles. For Commander Andy McEndrick, *Turbulent*'s commanding officer, the whole voyage was more than a job well done – it was a record breaker. From June 2002, *Turbulent* had been away more than ten months – a total of 300 days – travelling more than 50,000 miles, 40,000 of these being underwater, a record for the Royal Navy. Making passage out through the Red Sea, the temperature in the machinery space rose above 40 degrees. Much of the voyage is secret, part of the watching brief in the global anti-terrorist campaign after the attacks on 11 September 2001. *Turbulent* called at Diego Garcia, and ports in the Indonesian archipelago, always adapting to changes in orders and plans from headquarters at Northwood.

The high point was calling at the US base at Guam – 'the Japanese Ibiza' according to *Turbulent*'s crew – with nearly all 147 personnel booked into the same hotel. Sailing west towards Diego Garcia, the warning order was given to be ready for the Gulf, but this meant spending Christmas in Singapore. "We felt we were going back the wrong way," says McEndrick. The other low point came when the deployment started in the Northern Gulf in February, waiting for missiles and orders. "The atmosphere was really tense – we were there for a month," says McEndrick. "It was a question of management: keeping the guys ready to roll, but keeping a dampener on anticipation."

In a matter of days it was all over. The British Tomahawks were highly effective, matching the record of 100 per cent accuracy of the UK's new air-launched cruise, the Storm Shadow. Commander McEndrick had feared that the two systems might compete, even though they should be complementary, the submarine cruise missile having the advantage of near total surprise.

The job done, *Turbulent* got home on 16 April, to a "fantastic welcome." Of his company McEndrick says, "One hundred and forty-seven individuals, a huge range of personalities. Everybody made a contribution: it was a naval thing, a submarine thing. Every time they had to reach a peak, they made it. There were no passengers."

FROM THE COCKPIT

On 16 January, *HMS Cornwall* departed British waters to make all speed to Gibraltar. Aboard, Lieutenant Catherine Maley was the flight commander, with two Lynx helicopters which were about to discharge vital duties in the preparation of Operation Telic and the attack on Iraq.

For some time, intelligence had observed activity by cells of Al Qaeda sympathisers in Morocco. The narrow fast-running waters of the Straits of Gibraltar would be ideal ground for suicide attacks by small boats packed with explosive. In October 2000, a dinghy had exploded against the hull of the American destroyer *USS Cole* in Aden harbour, blowing a huge hole and killing 17 crew. A year later, the French tanker *Limburg* sustained a similar attack on the high seas not far from Aden; the tanker was crippled but no lives were lost.

A Royal Navy Merlin helicopter operating from RFA Fort Victoria in the Northern Arabian Gulf

Catherine Maley and her fellow aircrew had the task of 'Force Protection' – shepherding some 60 ships through the Straits of Gibraltar as they made their way across the Mediterranean to the Gulf via the Suez Canal. Gibraltar is a natural 'choke point' where any shipping is vulnerable to attack in the narrows. The passage to the Gulf is dotted with several 'choke points' where the Navy could be exposed to attack by suicide missions from land, sea or air: in the Suez canal itself; at Bab Al Mandab at the neck of the Red Sea; in the Straits of Hormuz; and in the tricky waters of the Northern Arabian Gulf. The Lynx helicopters of 815 Squadron would have a primary duty of force protection in these hot spots long after the main action of Operation Telic was over. The threat was real: an eight man Al Qaeda sabotage squad had been uncovered in Morocco, and, well into the Telic deployment, another group of Al Qaeda sympathisers had been rounded up in Spain.

After a rapid crossing of the Bay of Biscay ("pretty lumpy," according to Lt Maley), *HMS Cornwall* arrived in Gibraltar on 19 January. The aircrews were soon on patrol, the Mark 8 Lynx using its new radar, the Mark 3 employing its Night Vision aids. The main armament was a side-mounted M3M heavy machine-gun. "The ship would come up to heightened readiness. We would get airborne first in the Mark 8, followed by the Mark 3. Our job was to go ahead and relay pictures back to mother." 'Mother' at first was *HMS Cornwall*, later replaced by the Type 23 frigate *HMS Westminster*.

Above: *Flight Commander Lt Catherine Maley of the Naval Detachment to Gibraltar*
Below: *a Royal Navy Lynx helicopter from 815 Squadron*

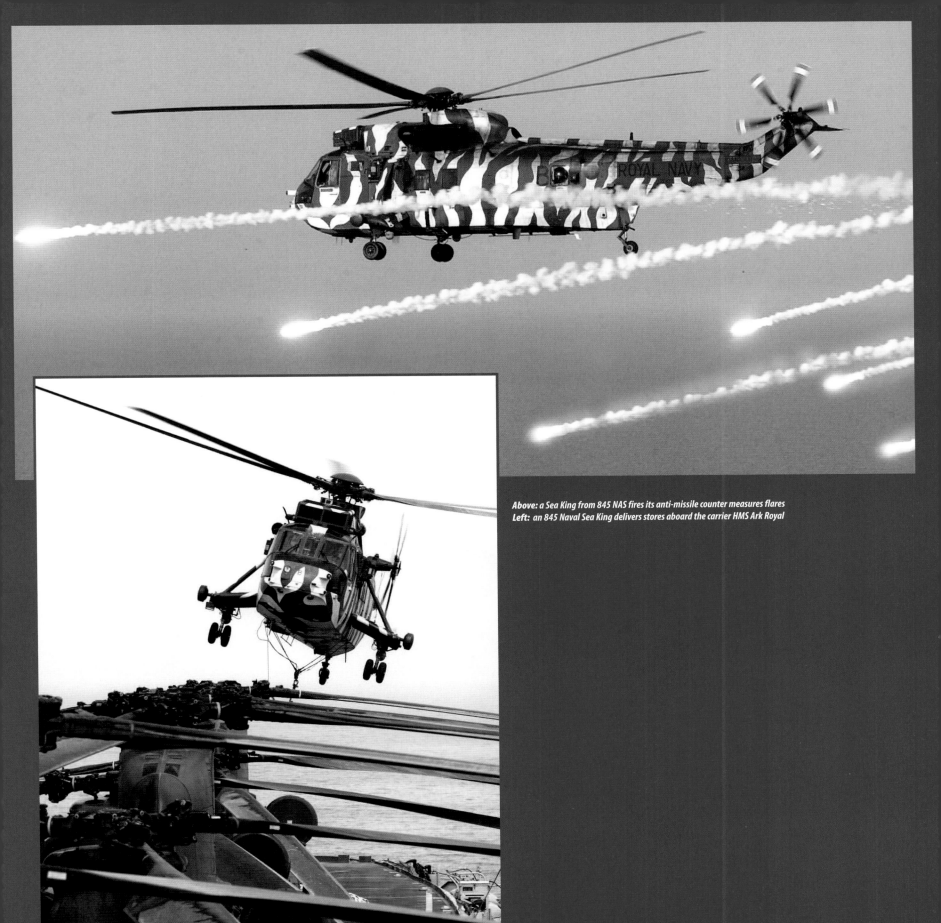

Above: a Sea King from 845 NAS fires its anti-missile counter measures flares
Left: an 845 Naval Sea King delivers stores aboard the carrier HMS Ark Royal

On the second sortie, Lt Maley and her crew spotted a speedboat ploughing down the straits towards *HMS Cornwall*. "She was heading for mother – so we tried to call on it to stop. It looked as if they might have a gunman in the back of the boat. We flew over it, covered it with our gun, and put ourselves between it and mother." After frantic hand gestures from the crew of the helicopter, the speedboat halted and then slipped off towards the coast as *Cornwall* passed.

The team from 815 Squadron shepherded more than 60 ships of Operation Telic from the Atlantic into the Mediterranean. Ships would bunch into small convoys, the fastest making the passage of the Gibraltar Narrows in under an hour. "We had to be ready at an hour's notice, day and night," recalls Lt Maley. "The waters were usually crowded with small boats, which could have hidden anything, and with the ferries to Morocco shuttling across at incredible speed."

It was a routine but necessary job, and is one of the key roles for the Navy today. For Catherine Maley, there was a small bonus: "When we were stationed abroad we resurrected the old Gibraltar Flight and I got the job of Flight Commander Gibraltar, which used to be a plum job. People back home were pretty envious."

Top: *a Sea King HS3 'Desert Duck' of the US Navy delivers mail and stores to RFA Sir Bedivere*
Above: *HMS Ark Royal in the Northern Arabian Gulf is resupplied by a Royal Navy Sea King Mk6 of 820 Squadron*

The view from the cockpit of a Sea King Mk4 towards another troop carrier from 845 NAS

Left: an 18 Squadron RAF Chinook lifts off from the deck of HMS Ark Royal towards Al Faw on another busy day of supplying ammunition ashore along with units of 845 NAS
Top: LAEMs Larry Holmes (left) and Matt Steele at work on an 847 Squadron Gazelle at temporary base 'Bonsai', near Umm Qasr
Above: victory in sight

The Naval Task Group drew on the services of some 48 helicopters during Operation Telic, carrying out a wide range of tasks, from surveillance to attack, and the delivery of troops and supplies in battle. Among them were the big RAF CH-47 Chinooks of 18 Squadron, which lifted 40 Commando into the Al Faw peninsula in the early hours of Friday 21 March; Lynx helicopters of 815 Squadron; and the Mk4 Sea Kings of 845 NAS, which together mounted patrols into hostile territory over Iraq and along the snaking waterways running into the Gulf. 'A' Flight of 849 Squadron mounted vital surveillance operations over land and sea from the decks of *HMS Ark Royal*. They kept going 24 hours a day, despite the terrible blow of losing two of their Sea King Mk7s in a mid-air collision in the early hours of 22 March.

Helicopters were scattered throughout the fleet, among them the new Merlin anti-submarine aircraft based with the *RFA Fort Austin*.

The assault
On 25 February, the Mk4 Sea Kings of 845 Naval Air Squadron carried out what was dubbed 'the mother of all rehearsals' in the northern Gulf. Lt Commander Jon Pentreath knew that his aircraft would have to carry out the key manoeuvre of the initial assault: to land the leading fighting elements of 40 Commando on the Al Faw peninsula.

The rehearsal went well, but a month later conditions did not seem so fair when the assault was about to go in for real on 20 March. "There was no contrast between land and sky," Pentreath remembers. "The moon was full but very dusty from the clouds of sand thrown up by the heavy armour moving towards the border. Flying into Iraq itself was a bit of a relief for the pilots as they could see much more clearly."

Top: an 18 Squadron RAF aircrewman waits as his aircraft is moved on to its spot for deployment ashore
Above: Leading Aircrewman Jason Bibby in a Sea King from 845 NAS

Flight operations at sea involved many different types of aircraft, including Lynx, Sea King, Merlin and Chinook helicopters

The first British officer to land was Lt Jason Blackwell RN, a fighter controller. He flew in with the US Navy Seals teams to prepare the landing sites for 845 Squadron and 40 Commando. With Corporal Andy Probert, he arrived on the scene well over an hour before the first Marine units. Crammed aboard an American MH-53 Sea Stallion, he recalls: "I saw nothing – I was too worried about being shot by the patrolling AC-130 Spectre gunship. There did seem to be more enemy than we had thought at first. I had expected the ground to be really firm, but it was ankle-deep mud."

A brisk firefight broke out by the military compound adjoining the oil pumping station which had been designated one of 40 Commando's first objectives. This died down after heavy firing from the gunship and the American assault party. In the main landing site stood a telegraph pole with wires running from it – a major hazard for any helicopter bringing in troops. The Chinooks of 18 Squadron were radioed to hold off while the landing team demolished the pole and wires. "We did it with three minutes to spare," says Jason Blackwell. The Sea Kings of 845 and Chinooks then maintained a constant shuttle landing men, weapons and stores.

Above, top right and bottom right: HMS Edinburgh's Lynx operating from the deck of HMS Ark Royal

Below: Leading Aircrewman Jason Bibby and a GPMG conduct door gunning in a Sea King from 845 NAS

The preparation for the landings had gone almost too well, and was nearly a victim of its own success. At 17 minutes before 'H' hour, a B 52 bomber was to drop precision guided bombs, JDAMs, to be followed minutes later by two AC130 gunships firing into the military base to stop any Iraqi forces preparing a counter-attack. This would be followed immediately by A10 tank busters putting down fire. The first bombs hit on time and on target, but raised so much sand that visibility for the helicopters as well as the fixed wing aircraft was reduced to nil. The operation was put on hold for half an hour.

Lieutenant Commander 'Sharky' Finn remembers flying nearly blind for most of the first night of the landings – and a blur of hectic activity in the days after, preparing the Marines to take Umm Qasr and ferrying ammunition and supplies for Operation James, the attack on Al Khasib and the final moves into Basra. Lt Gary Standen remembers the layers of sand on his Sea King ("thicker than snow") but he says his maintenance crews managed to keep the aircraft going despite the huge wear and tear of sand and dust on gearboxes and blades. Tail rotors had to be taped to protect them from sand. For air and engineering crew it was a 24/7 routine, and no one flagged. "One thing that sticks in my mind is that there was not a single case of an aircraft being flown incorrectly."

Top: a Sea King in the hover behind HMS Liverpool's Lynx
Above: a maintainer ties down a rotor blade of an 18 Squadron Chinook whilst a Sea King from 849 NAS approaches to land

Above: an aircrewman of 18 Squadron RAF checks that
his Chinook's wheels are clear as it lifts from the deck
Right: final approaches to the deck of HMS Ark Royal

Top: *a Lynx of 847 NAS lashed down onboard HMS Ocean*
Above: *Lynx helicopters depart from HMS Ocean to support troops ashore*

Not that the equipment worked perfectly. Sharky Finn remembered hearing of the CH-46 Sea Knight crash only seconds before getting airborne for the first assault. "I got to a hundred feet and couldn't see anything. The reflections from the desert into the atmosphere were blinding." Lt J. J. Hughes remembers relying on instruments all the way into enemy territory. "Crossing the border, I didn't feel scared, I felt comfortable. I hadn't seen the ground for half an hour, but as I got out over Bubiyan Island towards Al Faw I could see where I was going." Of the five hours flying he did that night, at least four and a half were done on instruments alone.

"I carried a lot of interesting loads over the next few weeks," says J. J. Hughes, "and sometimes met an interesting reception." His crewman Corporal Pat Patterson had to guide the Sea King in to pick up wounded prisoners of war between two sets of telephone wire. As the helicopter came in, the Iraqis opened up with mortars and machineguns. "I didn't know anything about it," says Patterson. On another occasion, J. J. Hughes felt the heat of a rocket round fired within inches of his cab. None of the helicopters was seriously damaged throughout the entire campaign, however. On the first night, one of the helicopters, piloted by Lt Vee (Victoria) Arden, was held in reserve as the radar altimeter was faulty. But all machines and crews flew throughout the operation – the most intense period of activity in the squadron's history.

The 'Killing Arm of the Navy'

"847 Squadron? It's the killing arm of the Royal Navy," says Captain Barney Barnwell, of the Royal Marines. With its six Lynx and six Gazelle helicopters, the squadron is the main attack helicopter force for the Royal Navy and Royal Marines. Barney himself is a Falklands veteran, serving in 40 Commando as an assault engineer in 1982. He became a pilot in 1986.

As the flight commander of the Gazelle force, he helped to develop the tactics for the light, manoeuvrable yet vulnerable aircraft to work with the more heavily armed and more durable Lynx. "In the battle area we worked a racetrack pattern, in and out over the targets, on patrol for over two hours at a time. The Gazelles found nine out of ten of the targets. They are less complicated than the Lynx and can spend more time searching. And they give less signature to the enemy."

Barney was flying as a pair with a Lynx piloted by Lt Commander Jim Newton, the squadron training officer, on the epic day of battle on 24 March. "All hell had broken loose. Every one of our patrols had been shot at. We knew that taxis had been driving in front of the enemy positions in the bunker and date palms, and spotting targets for the Iraqi artillery – so they were legitimate targets. I could see JDAM bombs detonating on the bunkers. The Scimitars of the Queen's Dragoon Guards (QDG) were shooting at anything. They had no artillery support."

Top: *a Gazelle takes off from HMS Ocean*
Above: *two Gazelles leave HMS Ocean to go ashore in Iraq*

The 847 helicopters ducked in and out over the targets, flying as low as ten feet off the ground to dodge missiles and anti-aircraft fire. Lt Andy Harcombe, who had only joined the squadron six months before, flew along the main road, calling in allied artillery fire. The helicopters had picked up a column of tanks and armoured personnel carriers, which had broken out of Basra to attack 40 Commando in the Faw peninsula.

"The QDG had reported contact across a wide front below us," recalls Lt Commander Jim Newton. "They said I was under fire." Barney Barnwell tried to guide me to a column of tanks about 1600 metres away." Newton fired the first TOW anti-tank missile at a command post where he had seen several Iraqis inside. "Seeing it hit was one of the low points, " he admitted later. A second missile was fired, as Barnwell saw one of the tanks train its gun on the helicopters. Then the

Above: a Gazelle helicopter shuts down at Umm Qasr
Below: an 845 Squadron Sea King on a 'recce' mission over the Al Faw peninsula

third missile hit a T-55 tank between the turret and chassis. "It blew up in a huge cloud of flame – much bigger than the JDAM bombs." Barney then trained his laser target control on another tank, and it too was destroyed by a TOW missile from the Lynx. "I had trained for this for years – but when it came to the real thing, I was surprised how close it all was. The tank I was targeting filled my screen. Working alongside Barney, well that's the only way to work."

On 30 March, in Operation James, Lt Commander Newton was the mission commander for the day, with Colour Sergeant Darby Allen as his pilot and Captain Dave 'Bunker' Abbott and Captain Mike Baker flying alongside. He was called in to investigate a transmitting station outside Al Khasib. Seeing an aerial sticking out above a bunker, he fired.

Through the operations on 24 and 30 March, the attack helicopters were called in to the targets by the QDG. Barney Barnwell distinctly remembers the cool and cultured tones of Major Henry Sugden. "He's really cavalry, but really calm and collected whenever he was calling us – even though he too

Above: a troop-carrying Sea King onboard HMS Ocean prepares for night operations
Below: a Chinook over the Northern Arabian Gulf ferries more supplies to the Al Faw peninsula

Above: a Sea King from HMS Ocean's embarked 845 Squadron, and a Chinook from 27 Squadron

In the afternoon of Operation James, Jim Newton returned the favour to the ground troops of 40 Commando and the QDG. The US-British forward observation party called up to say they could not see the target, a huge defensive bunker complex. The helicopters could see the bunker and gave the coordinates to the fire controllers of 29 Regiment Royal Artillery. "They fired one round 200 metres off target, and then adjusted and put down 68 rounds, all on target."

Petty Officer Audrey Stevenson was an airframes engineer, the only woman in the ground crew that kept the 847 helicopters flying. A former Harrier engineer, she volunteered for the helicopter teams to find a new challenge. The big challenge in Telic, she says, was sand. It got into the tents and the sleeping bags, and she had to cover her head with her bivvy bag when she slept. In the mornings she had to dig her way out. The sand meant that the rotor heads of the aircraft would have to be changed weekly. (In normal service, they are changed once or twice a year.) "We had to get good at it, quick."

"We worked our bollocks off," she says with a grin, in her mild Scots accent. "The air frames were phenomenally serviceable, and we had a good bit of luck with us. We didn't lose one aircraft. We did our job as 40 Commando did theirs on the ground. Happily my worst fears didn't happen – that things wouldn't succeed and I would let the lads down. My biggest worry is that I couldn't carry my Bergen, and be able to jump down from a helicopter with it. It's bigger and heavier than I am!

"After the Harriers I wanted a new challenge, and this was a challenge and a half. You must be careful what you wish for!"

Top: a Sea King Mk7 of 'A' Flight 849 Naval Air Squadron
Above: a member of the Royal Navy's mobile news team sets up to film onboard HMS Ark Royal

849 Squadron A Flight: Eyes Down

The four Sea King Mk7 helicopters of 849 Squadron joined *HMS Ark Royal* on 13 January. "We usually deploy with only three aircraft," says Lt Commander David Crimmen, the senior pilot. "This time we took four and eight crew because we knew there were likely to be operations for real." The Sea King 7s carry the latest ground and sea searching radar. They are the Navy's in-house AWACS – an early warning system developed in the Falklands campaign. Equipped with a new radar, the aircraft proved invaluable for sea and land operations in the opening phase of Operation Telic.

The Squadron began full 24 hour operations on 18 March, scanning the sea and coasts of Iraq. Four days later, at just after four in the morning, two of the Mk7s collided over the sea and all seven aboard were killed. Conditions had been poor, and air space had been crowded with flight paths tightly controlled for helicopters, strike aircraft and cruise missiles. The helicopters had been given a tight ceiling, particularly for cruise missile flights. One pilot in the campaign said he actually saw a Tomahawk missile flying over his helicopter.

The crash meant that 'A' Flight had lost seven out of its 24 officers. "It's a small unit, and this was a terrible blow," says David Crimmen. But within four hours, flying operations began again. "The brigadier said we had a real effect. He was worried about developments ashore and said we were needed."

Lt Commander Neal 'Stan' Hargreaves had helped to develop the new radars for the Sea Kings. They proved better than expected. "It has given us a capability we never had before, a real assistance to ground operations. It took this war to give us the final breakthrough in this capability.

"But the war brought the loss of some very good friends – it was shocking at the time, and still hasn't fully sunk in."

Stan Hargreaves also witnessed some of the worst flying conditions of his career, which embraces four campaigns. He was on patrol over the northern Gulf one night when a sandstorm swept in suddenly from the north. "The forecast had given no warning. I could see it coming and we turned south to get back to Ark Royal seven miles to the south. Then it just disappeared as the sand flew in. We had to find a deck with lights that could take us – none of the ships around could. Then we heard from the destroyer *USS Mileus*. When we approached, we knew she was making 15 knots and we hovered at 35 feet, and could not see a thing. Eventually we got down on the deck. We only had 50 lbs of fuel available – less than one minute's flying time."

ON THE GUNLINE

In the early hours of 21 March, *HMS Chatham* opened fire with her main gun on a designated target in the Al Faw peninsula. It was the first time a ship of the Royal Navy had undertaken a shore bombardment since the Falklands War almost 21 years earlier. A matter of minutes later, fire was called from the guns of the Type 23 frigates *HMS Marlborough* and *HMS Richmond*. Next to *Marlborough* in the gunline was the Australian frigate *HMAS Anzac*, which had fired the opening shot with her 5-inch gun.

In charge of the firing in *Chatham*'s Operations Room was Chief Petty Officer, CHOPS (M), David Farmer, who had discharged the same duties during the Falklands War in 1982, when he had controlled naval gunfire in the battles for Goose Green and Tumbledown. "The Mk8 gun is as good now as it was then – very accurate," he said with his soft Cornish accent. "The new 4.5-inch Mk8 Mod 1 gun in *HMS Marlborough* is even better. It's all been a lot easier this time."

Aircraft Engineering Mechanics maintain one of HMS Chatham's Lynx helicopters as part of Operation Resinate, the UK's ongoing commitment to patrol the Gulf for oil smugglers.

The Lynx helicopters are embarked as part of the Ship's Flight for her time in the Gulf, patrolling the region regularly for smugglers

The biggest worry, said the Chief, was the depth of the water – or, rather, the lack of it. He believed the fire missions – some 47 rounds in all from *Chatham* – had been completely accurate, taking out two military installations in 40 Commando's battle for Al Faw.

"But of course, it's a totally different Navy now." However, at 49, the Chief was not yet prepared to quit. He hoped to retire in his mid fifties.

HMS Chatham, a Type 22 Batch 3 frigate, larger than most in the fleet, had set sail with the main task group from Plymouth in January. It had been a busy deployment from the first day. The ship was to play a varied role in Operation Telic and was then switched to Operation Oracle – part of the open-ended campaign against terrorism. On the way, she escorted the nuclear-powered Tomahawk-firing submarine *HMS Splendid* through the Suez Canal.

HMS Marlborough, under the command of Captain Mark Anderson, led the naval gunfire flotilla. On the night of 21 March, he brought the ships forward to two firing areas, designated Juno and Sword after the code names for two of

Top: one of HMS Chatham's Operator Mechanics mans a GPMG as part of the ship's close protection team
Above: members of HMS Chatham working on the ship's charts

*Top: Signalman Bungy Williamson (of HMS Edinburgh) looks out from RFA Fort Victoria.
Royal Navy aircraft carrier HMS Ark Royal can be seen in the background*
*Above: HMS Richmond's 4.5-inch gun fires onto the Al Faw peninsula during Operation Telic.
Richmond was acting in support of Royal Marine Commandos in the region*
*Right: HMS Richmond, under the command of Commander Keble, closed up to action stations in
readiness to help secure the Iraqi coastline in support of coalition operations on the Al Faw peninsula*

the beaches at the D-Day landings in Normandy in June 1944. The gunfire drills and targets had been established by *Marlborough*'s Principal Warfare Officer, Lt Commander Craig Wood, in a series of meetings in *HMS Ocean*. Under the plan, *Marlborough*, *Chatham* and *Richmond* would fire initially in support of the operation by Bravo Company of 40 Commando. Fire was called from the shore by a team led by the Commander of 148 Battery.

The Americans were hesitant about using naval gunfire support – the local naval commander believed that it was better to call in air strikes. However, he was persuaded that naval gunfire would not be at the mercy of the weather as much as air power. This proved a good call: the weather was dreadful in the run-up to action and some of the air missions could not fly.

Top: *Operator Mechanic Jim Isherwood at sunset onboard HMS Edinburgh*
Above: *Operator Mechanics in HMS Chatham's Operations Room during a patrol of the Gulf*

HMS Chatham, a Type 22 frigate

Above: under stormy skies in the Northern Arabian Gulf. In the foreground, the destroyer HMS Edinburgh with (left to right) RFA Dilligence; RFA Argus, a Sir Class LSL; and the destroyer HMS Liverpool in the background
Below: HMS Marlborough on fast passage to the Northern Arabian Gulf

"The support was tremendous," says Captain Anderson. "It worked very well." Unlike the Falklands experience, none of the radio links between ships and shore went down. In 36 hours the ships put down 155 rounds. The Battery Commander reported that "Success on the Al Faw was due to the aggressive use of indirect fire support, especially the swift response from NGS ships, which had a huge impact on the ground and shattered the enemy's will to fight." Some missions only involved single shots to force groups of Iraqi soldiers to surrender.

Aboard the frigates of the gunline, life could be quite crowded and cramped. *Marlborough* was at defence watches for 53 days. *Chatham* had an augmented company with a Royal Marine party aboard and crews for two Lynx helicopters. Cabins below the water line had to be given up for safety reasons (because of the mine threat). Mattresses were laid down in messes and 52 slept in the wardroom. Some had to 'hot bunk' (i.e. take turns to sleep in the same bunk).

HMS Liverpool manoeuvring

Top: *HMS Liverpool patrols the Northern Arabian Gulf*

Above: *Operator Mechanic Gary Keen and Leading Operator Mechanic 'Hoppy' Hopkins test HMS Ocean's 20mm guns as she sails into the Mediterranean*

Flying forward from the ships, the Lynx helicopters of 815 Squadron became their eyes as they scoured the river estuaries for any suspicious shipping, minelayers and, possibly, suicide boats. The ships on the gunline had the fear of Iraqi Seersucker surface-to-surface missiles being fired from the shore, and at least two were loosed off in the general direction of Kuwait. Lieutenants Lee Kennington and Toby Clay pursued and photographed an Iraqi Type 15 launch which had more than a dozen mines concealed beneath tarpaulins. More of the craft, and mines, were found in Umm Qasr. Toby Clay thought the Iraqis may have been on the point of laying mines, but then thought better of it.

Sub Lieutenant Amy Dobson was awarded her wings in September 2002. By March 2003, she was patrolling the Gulf in one of *Chatham*'s Lynx helicopters. The crew consisted of a pilot, observer, and door gunner manning the .5 calibre M3M heavy machinegun. "It was completely different from training, because we had such a small area to patrol, a box 15 miles by 15 miles." Two days before the war broke out, one of *Chatham*'s Lynx saw a huge flotilla of more than fifty dhows coming down the waterways, heading for the open sea. "They were flying white flags. I was in the back with the gun loaded. They were just trying to get away, and I don't blame them. They knew what was coming and they wanted to leave – for which I had quite a bit of sympathy."

Chatham had another powerful weapon aboard: two transmitters churning out pop music and messages about how to surrender. Similar messages were deployed in the millions of leaflets dropped all over Iraq. Captain the Hon. Michael Cochrane, *Chatham*'s commanding officer, says he was not entirely sure about the content of the broadcasts, but he believes they did have an effect. "People did come up waving the leaflets, asking to surrender."

By May, *Chatham* was again on patrol as 'eyes and ears', searching for Al Qaeda links across a sweep of the Arabian Sea and the Indian Ocean – in which she had some notable successes. "It is really vital work," says Michael Cochrane, "in which we link up with the ships of a large coalition in these waters." He believes his young crew (with an average age in the low 20s) had learned a lot from their hectic days in Operation Telic. "It was great watching some highly individual people learning a lot about themselves, and realising that they really could do it."

Above: Sub Lieutenant Amy Dobson mans the M3M Heavy Machine Gun on HMS Chatham's Lynx
Below: the Reverend Caroline Eglin, Chaplain on the Type 42 destroyer HMS Edinburgh, takes the Sunday Service, where the Banns of marriage were read for Leading Steward Nicholas 'Digger' Gardner's engagement to Elodie Yates
Bottom: Operator Mechanic Lee Mears keeps a look out

THE BIG SHIPS
AND THEIR ESCORTS

Leading the Navy's task group were the two carriers *HMS Ark Royal* and *HMS Ocean*. Both were in the role of Commando helicopter carriers. It was a role for which *Ark Royal* was not originally designed and a role into which *HMS Ocean* had already evolved in its short history. Between them they could land almost a commando's worth of assault troops by helicopter, and possibly more by landing craft.

By the time the flagship *Ark Royal* reached the Gulf, she had 1,300 sailors, aviators and Marines aboard. On 11 January she was ordered to deploy. The captain, Alan Massey, was worried that the ship was being asked to do so without being fully ready to go: "It is quite an elaborate change round to convert from flying fixed-wing aircraft to becoming a helicopter assault ship." Captain Massey – and the news channels on the ship's television – made sure that the ship's company was kept informed about the international situation. In the deep loch at Glenmalen in Scotland, the ship took on stores and ammunition in quantity – a sure sign that she was going to war.

An Operator Mechanic at action stations

A few days later, the Sea King Mk7s of 849 Squadron and the Chinooks of 18 Squadron embarked. By mid February, *Ark Royal*, followed by *Ocean*, was in the Gulf, in time for full rehearsals for the attack on Al Faw. Moving into the northern Gulf, *Ark Royal* had to ride at anchor, protected by her escort, the Type 42 destroyer *HMS Liverpool*. Accompanying *Ocean* was another Type 42, *HMS Edinburgh*. "No other water space was available to us," says Captain Massey. "We felt very uncomfortable. The weather was bad, and the forecasting was not all accurate."

Ark Royal had been assigned what Captain Massey termed "a discreet job." With *Ocean* she was to get as close to the Iraqi coast as possible in order to support the troops ashore – a huge risk because of the shallowness of the water and the perpetual risk of mines, suicide boats and anti-ship missiles. Within a day of the operation starting, two helicopters, one inbound and the other outbound from *Ark Royal*, collided. "Everybody knew what had happened within an hour. The mood was a complete contrast to what it had been a day before. Now people were meeting in disconsolate huddles. Just 24 hours into the mission and the ship had gone completely silent. Not long after, we heard of the loss of the Tornado over Kuwait."

Above: *HMS Liverpool in the Northern Arabian Gulf (foreground), in company with HMS Ocean and HMS Edinburgh*
Below: *a school of dolphins swimming freely in front of HMS Ocean*

Above: two Landing Craft Vehicle and Personnel (LCVPs) from 9 Assault Squadron Royal Marines (9ASRM), which were embarked in HMS Ocean, pass aircraft carrier HMS Ark Royal and the Type 42 destroyer HMS Liverpool
Right: HMS York patrols in the evening haze

The crash appeared to deepen the commitment of the ship's company to the mission, particularly 849 Squadron. "They were soon flying again as they knew they had an absolutely indispensable role," says Massey. The day after Baghdad fell, *Ark Royal* pulled out of the northern Gulf. "Against the odds we had done the job of a helicopter assault ship, landing Delta Company of 40 Commando on the Al Faw peninsula. We had a lot of youngsters, who were pretty scared at times."

Great care was taken to allow free phone calls and access to e-mail. Above all, Alan Massey praises the 150 female crew he had aboard: "A real force multiplier. They are often more natural and effective and can make the boys work harder. They look out for each other, and don't keep things bottled up."

Following *Ark Royal*'s every move was *HMS Liverpool*, her escort or 'sheep dog'. Commander Martin Ewence, commanding *HMS Liverpool*, said his job was always to be "one and a half miles up threat from *Ark Royal*. It was better for me to be hit. If the *Ark Royal* had been struck, it would have been a disaster."

Top: HMS Liverpool in the Northern Arabian Gulf

Above: the Naval Task Group in the Mediterranean prior to transit through the Suez Canal

Above: replenishment at sea
Left: HMS Marlborough in the Northern Arabian Gulf, in company with the USS Mobile Bay

Below: Operation Cyprus Wader. 27 Squadron and HMS Ocean's Tailored Air Group (845 & 847 NAS) take 40 Commando Royal Marines ashore

Bottom: Landing Craft Vehicle Personnel (LCVP) from 9 ASRM deliver stores during Operation Cyprus Wader

Top: A Sea King Mk6 of 820 NAS transfers stores to Ark Royal from RFA Fort Austin

Middle: HMS Ark Royal in the Northern Arabian Gulf

Above: HMS Edinburgh during Operation Telic

The main fear was attack by suicide boat or seersucker missile, of which a number were fired in late March, with more found near Umm Qasr. "It was very exciting as there was a constant air threat," says Commander Ewence. *Liverpool* was given the task of coordinating air defence for the whole UK Task Group – a busy period for her Operations Room. No-one was allowed to sleep in accommodation below the waterline due to the threat from mines.

As Liverpool was called to action stations on the night of 20 March, she moved into the assault lanes, protecting Ark Royal as Delta Company of 40 Commando were lifted from her decks. "It was a long night and we had to keep people awake and interested. At 2300 we distributed Mars bars and orange juice. I talked to Captain Massey in *Ark Royal* and we decided to serve breakfast at one in the morning." A day later the ship ran out of crisps and – with crew morale in mind – the Lynx was dispatched to Kuwait to buy every packet of crisps in sight.

By the end of April, *Liverpool* parted from her charge and with *HMS Marlborough* sailed for the Pacific to resume a programme of preplanned exercises in South East Asia.

"Ocean has never followed the fleet programme," explains her captain, Adrian Johns. "She has never finished a deployment as intended." She had been commanded by Captain Johns in Operation Jacana, in which most of 45 Commando was launched from her decks into Afghanistan. In the work-up, the Marines ran firing practices off the side and used the central deck as an assault course, while helicopter operations continued at the opposite end of the deck.

Above: HMS Edinburgh on patrol in the Northern Arabian Gulf
Below: 40 Commando Royal Marines load Land Rovers and quad bikes into Chinooks

Above: HMS Liverpool carries out evasive manoeuvres with its own ship's boat acting as an 'enemy threat'
Left: HMS Ocean transits the Suez Canal as she heads home from the Gulf and Operation Telic. Operator Mechanic Claire Davidson mans the 20mm Gambo Gun, with Operator Mechanic Andrea Spurs assisting as lookout

Above: HMS Ark Royal in the Northern Arabian Gulf, off Kuwait City
Below: Royal Marines of Delta Company 40 Commando make final preparations

By mid February planning began with the local American HQ. "We were getting an intelligence reach that we didn't know existed." It was decided that the primary assault should come from Kuwait, with one company being lifted off the decks of the carriers. On the night of 20 March the ship went to action stations. "It brought home reality for the first time – I looked round and watched people doing what they had always been trained to do. It was a surreal experience because, with the crash of the CH-46 helicopter, the timeline slipped. Once we knew they had established a foothold on Al Faw, we waited for the next step, and prepared for casualties."

In the space of 72 hours, 355 deck movements were made from *Ocean* alone – shifting pallets of ammunition for the mortar troops, who were breaking open the pallets as they landed. "The pace didn't slacken. *HMS Edinburgh* was with us constantly, and did not go alongside in 100 days."

Captain Johns left the ship at the end of April to become Assistant Chief of the Naval Staff as a Rear Admiral. He knew it had been his final job at sea. "To have commanded a ship like *Ocean* in two major operations and see it come together – I couldn't have scripted it. I left on a complete professional high. I was only sorry I could not bring the ship home."

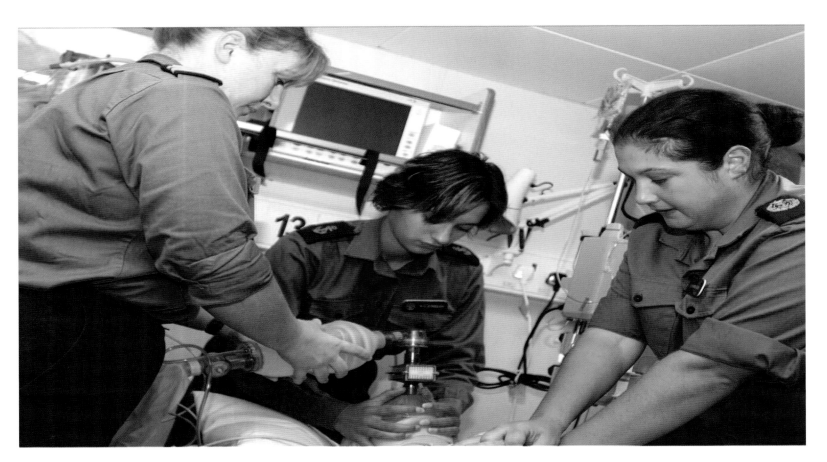

LIFE SUPPORT MACHINE

"Our job was to get as close to the front line as possible and we had to be prepared for chemical attack." As a job description, this sounds pretty challenging but it is how Surgeon Commander Liz Nichols describes the missions of the teams of the Commando Forward Surgical Groups (CFSGs).

With the Commando Brigade seven surgeons and seven doctors worked from two operating tables. "We had to be really manoeuvrist, be truly part of an amphibious operation." The surgical teams had to carry their own equipment, with the support of only a tracked ambulance. They also had to fill the gaps for other units – the Americans' 15 Marine Expeditionary Unit (MEU) had no dedicated medical facility. The doctors and nurses had to dig holes in the desert and clear buildings littered with ammunition and detritus to set up their operating theatres.

Commander Nichols knew the two surgical teams would be severely tested when it came to major action in the advance towards Umm Qasr and Operation James, the move onto Al Khasib, and the approach to Basra. In all, the CFSG teams treated 250 casualties in just over a fortnight. Of these, ten were heavily traumatised battle casualties and 195 were 'Role 2', that is, in danger of dying within two hours if they were not treated. Every one of the casualties brought to the medical teams survived.

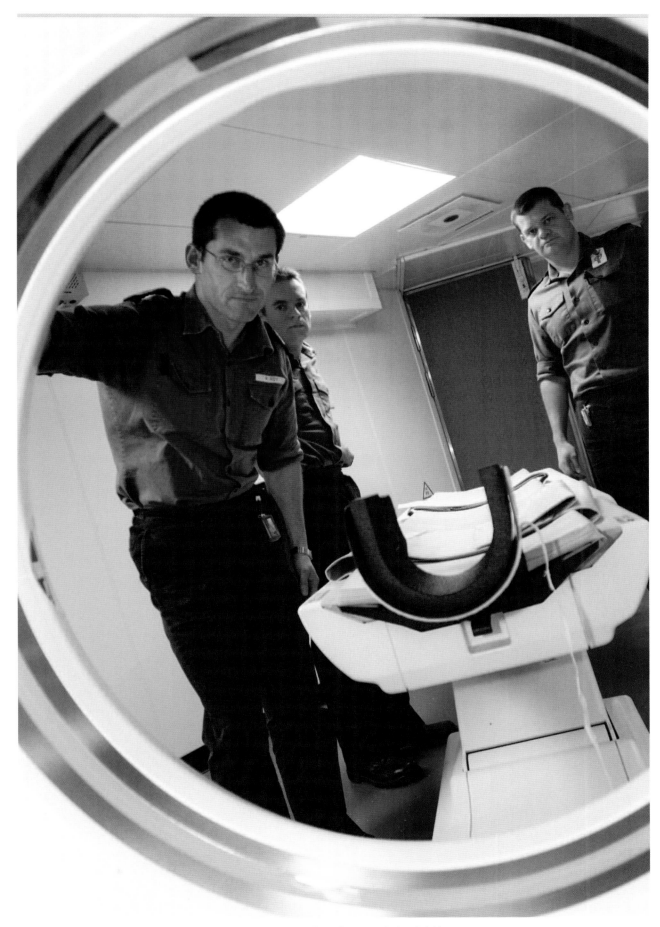

Onboard RFA Argus in the Northern Arabian Gulf. **Above**: the staff of the CT scanner, headed by Chief Petty Officer Adan Roy (Radiographer), left

Opposite: naval nurses (from left to right) Lt Elaine Thorpe, Leading Naval Nurse Nicky D'Mello and Chief Petty Officer Louise Spellor carry out resuscitation training

"It was pretty hectic," says Commander Nichols, recalling the casualties from Operation James. "The conditions were much harsher than expected but the guys adapted." Liz Nichols believes that her teams have pioneered ways of operating much closer to the front line than before – with useful lessons, perhaps, for the Army's airmobile units, and aid agencies in the field. "The aim is surgical resuscitation and intervention. It's 'Casualty' up the sharp end."

One of the Accident and Emergency specialists up the sharp end was Lt Leah Chilvers, a specialist A&E nurse with the Regimental Aid Post of 42 Commando. She remembers days of living in holes in the desert, and manpacking most of her medical kit on her back, though occasionally an RM BV tracked vehicle did come to help. Shortly after landing, her unit came under artillery bombardment on the Al Faw: "I think that was the low point," she says. "I had to work as an individual – and there was no staff. It was a war situation." Leah is credited by colleagues with one of the most remarkable medical feats of Operation Telic: she fitted a cavity drain into a badly traumatised Iraqi casualty near Umm Qasr. The patient survived.

Above: RFA Sir Bedivere encounters a sandstorm in the Arabian Gulf, reducing visibility considerably. A lookout is forced to wear a dust mask

Below: repairs to RFA Argus in the Northern Arabian Gulf. MV Passat sits alongside for cranage

Top: Argus's Nurse in Charge, Lt Commander Steve Spencer QARRNS (Queen Alexandra's Royal Naval Nursing Service) is shown on a High Dependency Ward

Above and Right: Medical teams from 42 Commando, Derriford Hospital and other attached units practise setting up and running frontline medical tents. Training involves preparing for any possible situation which the medics could be faced with in the field, from a chemical attack to an ingrowing toenail. The medical teams took part in a two-day exercise in Camp Gibraltar and adjoining camps in Kuwait, and worked some very long hours, but always had a smile for the patients who were brought in

Many of the casualties were taken by helicopter to the Royal Fleet Auxiliary *Argus*, the Navy's helicopter training ship with a brand new surgical facility on three decks, and boasting some of the latest facilities, including a CAT scan.

In *Argus* (a veteran from the Falklands where she traded as a freighter under the name *Contender Bezant*), a surgical team of 80 had assembled in January. "It was all a bit of a shock," says Commander Judy Onions of the Queen Alexandra's Royal Naval Nursing Service, the Matron aboard *Argus*. Some of her team had only been in the Navy for a few months. As *Argus* made her way to the Gulf, the medical teams carried out practices and rehearsals, including a trial with US helicopters to test whether they could handle 20 major casualties at a time. So impressed were the Americans that one swore he would immediately get a new tattoo stating 'if injured send to *Argus*.'

Top: *RFA Fort Rosalie, RFA Sir Percivale and HMS Ocean*
Above: *The flight deck of RFA Sir Percivale is cleared to receive stores*

Above: *RFA Bayleaf conducts a Replenishment at Sea (RAS) with HMS Edinburgh in the company of coalition warships*

Below: *RFA Grey Rover, RFA Diligence, and HMS York 'rafted up' in the Arabian Gulf*

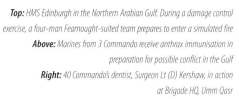

Top: HMS Edinburgh in the Northern Arabian Gulf. During a damage control
exercise, a four-man Fearnought-suited team prepares to enter a simulated fire
Above: Marines from 3 Commando receive anthrax immunisation in
preparation for possible conflict in the Gulf
Right: 40 Commando's dentist, Surgeon Lt (D) Kershaw, in action
at Brigade HQ, Umm Qasr

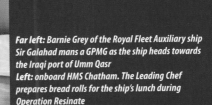

Far left: Barnie Grey of the Royal Fleet Auxiliary ship Sir Galahad mans a GPMG as the ship heads towards the Iraqi port of Umm Qasr
Left: onboard HMS Chatham. The Leading Chef prepares bread rolls for the ship's lunch during Operation Resinate
Below: 'Clicky' McCullen (left) and 'Stan' Matthews (right) backed up by their team leader during fire-fighting training onboard HMS Ocean

As the tempo of action quickened, the *Argus* teams were receiving casualties for six hours at a stretch. By this time they had 100 beds, ten of them for the most seriously wounded. They received victims of the friendly fire incidents with the British tanks outside Basra. Most of the wounded were Iraqis, among them children. "We were always ready for incoming," says Commander Onions, "whether it was casualties or ordnance."

In mid April the surgical teams flew home, their job done. "It was a very good team. It gelled. And it was very well planned."

Watching the surgeons at work was "a humbling experience," says Captain Bob Allan of the Royal Fleet Auxiliary, the commanding officer of *Argus*. "There was a real buzz as they worked – and they had vast knowledge and experience."

"*Argus* really proved herself," adds Captain Allan. "I am glad she remained grey."

"Glad to be grey" may not sound the most dynamic of slogans, but being grey and not white, *Argus* remains a 'ship of the line' of the Navy. It means she can go forward into the battle zone as the primary casualty reception centre. If she were a hospital ship she would be painted white with red crosses, and would be restricted by the Geneva Convention. What's more, she would be kept out of combat areas as far as possible. (The US hospital ship *USS Comfort*, by contrast, had to stay in the southern end of the Gulf.)

Captain Allan had a company of more than 400 aboard, including the Marine Band, 820 Squadron with five Sea King helicopters, logisticians and a naval party. He has particular praise for the band: "They weren't just stretcher bearers but medical logisticians trained in the techniques of biological and chemical weapons decontamination. They were terrific."

Some 500 casualties were treated in *Argus* and then passed to hospitals ashore. Two cases remain in Rob Allan's memory. An Iraqi boy had a bullet in his head. The neurosurgeon managed to remove the bullet, and the boy survived. So too did a 12-year-old Iraqi who had a bullet lodged near his liver. Using the CAT scan, the surgeons managed to locate the bullet. "They partially operated on the wound, allowed it to heal and then operated again," recalls the captain.

Royal Fleet Auxiliary
The *Argus* is one of the leading ships of the Royal Fleet Auxiliary, which had two thirds of its fleet committed to Operation Telic: ammunition ships, freighters, ancient oilers from the sixties and the floating repair dock *RFA Diligence*, which did to ships what the medical teams did to human casualties. Another famous name was that of the Landing Ship Logistic *Sir Galahad*, which had been built to replace the old Galahad hit at Fitzroy in the Falklands and now a war grave.

Aboard the new *Galahad* were 350 Marines as well as Army logisticians. "I had to make life as comfortable as possible," says the commanding officer, Captain Roger Robinson-Brown. "It was very easy to get people motivated – the average age of my deck party was 50.8 – the best men to have around."

Towards the end of March, *Sir Galahad* was allocated the task of being the first ship to take aid into Iraq. "The job came up at Umm Qasr and I was privileged to do this." The task carried huge risks from mines and sudden ambushes by suicide boats. A dinghy fitted with explosives and rockets had been found by the waterfront near Umm Qasr. Three dinghies were tracked coming down the Shatt al Arab, and it is thought that the Iranians seized at least one of them. The *Sir Galahad* had to negotiate a channel only 250 metres wide and at four knots – the speed of the minehunters, led by *HMS Sandown*, ahead of her. "I was ready to go for it, but it was difficult – it was easy to be blown off course at that speed." The minehunting teams found two mines recently and expertly laid by the channel.

Top: medical teams from 42 Commando, Derriford Hospital and other attached units in a frontline medical tent during a two-day exercise in Kuwait
Above: a doctor attends to an Iraqi patient onboard the Principal Casualty Receiving Ship (PCRS) RFA Argus

Umm Qasr and Az Zubayr further inland proved an eye-opener for Captain Robinson-Brown. "It was really terrifying to see the amount of munitions just lying about the place."

His abiding impression, he says, is of the resilience of his crew of 55 men. "I was really impressed how they responded, considering we had a 30% crew change – in keeping with RFA practice."

Operation Telic was in fact the biggest deployment for the Royal Fleet Auxiliary since the Falklands. The scale of the challenge was awesome. "Replenishment at sea is our main business – and we do it better than anyone," says the RFA chief Commodore Peter Lannin. He is particularly proud of the new support systems for families and men and women at sea, chat rooms, e-mails, 24-hour help lines, and regular meetings of regional families' associations. This, with a special 'RFA allowance' for deployment of £187 a month, has done wonders for recruitment and morale.

"They are all volunteers: civilians prepared to work under real threat and danger. We didn't have to force anyone. They did a really good job, were very well organised, and they were manning some old ships, which has its own risks.

"Once again, the RFA did everything asked of it."

FIRST IN LAST OUT

The first naval units to arrive in the Gulf to prepare for Operation Telic were the minehunters, and they were among the last to leave. A flotilla of six minehunters – *Sandown*, *Brocklesby*, *Blyth*, *Grimsby*, *Ledbury* and *Bangor* – had been assigned to a series of exercises with the Americans, Saudis and Omanis as part of the Armilla patrols. Early in the new year, however, the mine-hunters and their command ship *RFA Sir Bedivere* were 'chopped', or switched to the command of the American mine task group under Commodore Mike O'Moore in the *USS Ponce*.

Their prime task would be to clear the Khawr abd Allah (KAA) and the Shatt al Arab to give access to Umm Qasr and Basra. But the first enemy proved to be the weather. "The KAA was very difficult for us. We had horrendous sandstorms, and 50 to 60 knot winds," recalls the commanding officer of *HMS Sandown*, Lt Cdr (now Commander) Gavin Young. "It was Gulf weather at its most extreme."

Above: HMS Ledbury

The minehunters split into three teams: the ships commanded by Commander Charlie Wilson working with separate US teams of divers with (real) dolphins, and MH-53 Sea Stallions. The helicopters would drive down the waterways first, trailing sleds to detect any explosives in and around the water.

The two biggest hazards were free-floating mines and tethered mines – of which there was plenty of evidence in boats and sheds up and down the river coasts. "Once identified we blew the thing up. We left no doubt," says Commander Young. An added hazard was the ordnance left behind by the previous wars along Al Faw, and the dozens of wrecks in the sea and in the waterways. Gavin Young said he was glad to have a party of Royal Marines aboard. "They helped to look out for the threat from suicide boats and could check the dhows of smugglers which came down the rivers."

Sandown was given the honour of the delicate manoeuvre of leading *Sir Galahad* into Umm Qasr. Gavin Young says he was particularly grateful for his crew. "Some were very young, but one or two were three badge long-service men."

Leading Chef Paul O'Neill became something of a magician. "It wasn't just bog-standard pies and chips, but he did Chinese and Indian as take-aways – and was a master at recycling food. He was good and very amusing, day in, day out for ten months." The Marine Engineering Officer Charge Chief Duncan Payne was also an influence. "I wouldn't say we had become a psychiatric ward, but he kept people going. He just kept tabs on people."

Above: *Umm Qasr port at sunset*

Below: *Royal Fleet Auxiliary ship Sir Galahad arrives in the port of Umm Qasr after Mine Counter Measure Vessels had cleared the way*

Top: *US Mine Counter Measures Vessel (MCMV) in the Arabian Gulf* **Above and right:** *a Royal Navy MCMV, one of six sent to the Northern Arabian Gulf, investigates a contact on the seabed. A remotely piloted vehicle is sent down. On this occasion the contact is nothing more than debris. On 15 March 2003, three members of the British press were transferred from RFA Sir Bedivere to HMS Brocklesby for a morning of demonstrations of the ship's role as an MCMV. Two of the press men were from the ITN news network and the third was from The Sun newspaper. They were given a tour of the ship, followed by a demonstration by the ship's mine clearance divers and the mine detection and demolition systems*

Coordinating the minehunters for the US as well as the UK was Commander Charlie Wilson. In all he had 10 minesweepers under his command, plus an extra two which joined later from the UK. He brought the ships in after the helicopters had done the "precursor influence sweeping." Once found, any ordnance would be blown up, usually by the British remote-controlled vessels, the SWIMs.

First into the KAA, 10 kilometres ahead of the rest, was *HMS Brocklesby*. She had the lowest 'signature' – and was the least likely to detonate a mine. More than 80 'Manta' mines were found in a row close to the main shipping lane. The specialist detonator was *HMS Blyth*, as she had just received a brand new 'one shot' device under the emergency purchase procedure for Operation Telic. "It was bought off the shelf – but was very effective," says Commander Wilson.

Top: *divers from Fleet Diving Unit in the port of Umm Qasr searching the waters for mines and explosives left by Iraqi forces before occupation*
Inset: *Petty Officer Diver Si Marston gives the thumbs up, Umm Qasr*
Above: *L/Corporal Rich Jones of 71 Port Maritime Regiment mans a GPMG onboard the RFA Sir Galahad as she heads towards Umm Qasr. Sir Galahad was the first to arrive in the port after the start of the war*

GENERAL COMPANY FOR PORTS OF IRAQ
UM-QASSIR PORT CRANE NO. 03

الشركة العامة لموانئ العراق
ميناء أم قصر رافعة رقم 03

Left: a Royal Marine from 3 Commando Brigade keeps a watchful eye over the port of
Umm Qasr prior to the arrival of humanitarian aid onboard RFA Sir Percivale
Below: HMS Brocklesby during mine clearance operations off the Iraqi port of Umm Qasr.
A US Coast Guard boat patrols nearby

Above: minehunter HMS Bangor
Right: RFA Sir Galahad heads towards Umm Qasr with minesweeper
HMS Sandown (leading) to deliver humanitarian aid to the people of Iraq

During the breakthrough operation into the KAA, the minehunters were hit by a four day sandstorm. Soon after the main action began, *HMS Grimsby* was detached for the sad duty of recovering the bodies from the Sea King crash of 849 Squadron.

Charlie Wilson takes pride that not a single ship was lost to a mine, though there were plenty of mines about. "We worked very well with the Americans. The training and the personnel were outstanding. They responded to all threats such as the suicide boats. And the equipment stood up very well, particularly our sonars. We must also mention the RFA, for with *Sir Bedivere* I had a really good forward HQ dedicated to mine warfare."

Is Britain still a leader in countermine operations? "Like Manchester United, we're not guaranteed to win, but we'll always be there, or thereabouts."

Above: HMS Sandown during mine clearance operations off the Iraqi port of Umm Qasr. An Australian Sea King patrols overhead

Below: RFA Sir Bedivere at dawn

Leading Marine Engineering Mechanic George Clough and friend with Saddam Hussein in Az Zubayr

STAND DOWN

By late April, many of the forward ships and units were heading out of the Gulf for other assignments and duties, and some to go home. The routine of the previous months had been testing, and exhausting. Ships' companies had been on defence watches (six hours on, six hours off) for nearly two months. And there had been the constant threat of missiles, possibly with biological or chemical warheads, and suicide boats. The men of Bravo Company 40 Commando had to yomp for 15km to the line of departure for Operation James and go into action for 19 hours to take Al Khasib and the approaches to Basra.

Going home, the ships gradually returned to a more normal routine: maintenance, exercises, and some sport. Mothers' Day was celebrated by a few of the ships in alternative nautical style as the ships headed away from the combat zone in the Gulf and the Arabian Sea.

On land the Marines and soldiers found time for sport. Impromptu football matches were staged with local teams on the baked hard mud of the village football pitches – an enjoyable pastime and important in building the relationship with the Iraqis. Some units used the hardened sand for cricket.

The helicopter crews of 845 Squadron, at ten minutes' call round the clock from their forward position near Az Zubayr, found an ingenious way to keep their mates alert and on the ball. Each crew departing on a mission set their successors on the ground a challenge; first it was to build outdoor furniture, then a sunshade, a rock garden and finally a fully functioning water feature driven by an old pump from one of Saddam's arsenals.

Those returning home were reunited with family and friends, with at least some of their thoughts still with colleagues who remained on duty in the Gulf and Iraq, and those who had died.

Left: some much-needed football practice at Camp Gibraltar in the Kuwait desert shortly before the start of the operation
Below: Marines of Juliet Company 42 Commando play a local Iraqi side in a friendly game of football

Marines take part in the Memorial Half Marathon in the naval base at Az Zubayr to commemorate comrades lost during the conflict

This page: Memorial Half Marathon,
Az Zubayr naval base

Top and right: Marines playing volleyball and rugby, Az Zubayr naval base, Iraq

Marines from 42 Commando consider their next move. The game is 'Uckers', a traditional naval board game

Clockwise from left: *taking the strain onboard HMS Ocean; crew onboard HMS Ark Royal watch a live news broadcast of the ship's captain; making the most of some time out in a popular naval fashion by staging 'flight deck sports,' including 'human skittles' and 'It's a Knockout'; and "Happy Mothers' Day" from HMS Ocean*

*Above and right: a short distance from home, sailors in HMS Ocean rekindle their allegiance to their football teams, Newcastle United and Sunderland; **Bottom right:** Portsmouth Football Club supporters onboard HMS Ark Royal send a message of support to their team from the Northern Arabian Gulf, Saturday, 5 April 2003, before watching the team's 2–1 win over Walsall live on the carrier. From left to right, Chief Petty Officer Neil Theuma, Chief Petty Officer Nigel Pead, Leading Air Engineering Mechanic Kev Alexander, and Petty Officer Phil Enright **Below:** HMS Ocean's Scottish Six – back row (from left to right), LMAQ Angie Moore, Writer Laura Connell, Chef Kelly Gillies, LMEM Daisy Adams; front row (from left to right), Writer Cheryl Mitchell, Steward Karen Green*

Above: HMS Splendid flies the Jolly Roger
(the sign of a successful naval mission),
completing her last-ever operational voyage,
17 July 2003
Right: minehunters return to Portsmouth

Top: HMS Ark Royal returns to her naval base of Portsmouth, welcomed home by wellwishers and families of her crew on Saturday, 17 May 2003

Right: Chef David Muir from HMS Blyth greets his
twin daughters Kimberley and Rebecca, aged 3
Below: HMS Ocean returns to Devonport

REFLECTIONS

The major combat phase of Operation Telic lasted little more than three weeks, from 19 March to 9 April. To within a day or two it was of the same duration as the land operations in the Falklands campaign in 1982 – though the sea battle in the Falklands lasted twice as long.

There could not have been a greater contrast, in setting, climate, and threat, between Operation Telic – the battle for Iraq – and Operation Corporate – the recovery of the Falklands. Doubtless, as after the Falklands, the wiseacres will say there will never be an operation or campaign quite like the one fought in Iraq through the spring and summer of 2003. No campaign is ever quite the same as any other: look at the difference between Operation Granby, the 'Desert Storm' campaign to free Kuwait from Saddam's clutches (where the Navy was also deeply involved), and Operation Telic. Lessons will be learned, as they always are, and all those in the Royal Navy will reflect on their achievements in the Northern Gulf and Iraq in 2003.

Any first observation must be the speed with which the naval forces led by the Amphibious Task Group and the Royal Marines of 3 Commando Brigade prepared and deployed. This is a testament to the quality of the people in the services, and the training they received. The Navy and its Marines acted as part of a coalition in which the Americans were the senior partners.

The ability of British forces to operate successfully with their coalition partners was fully tested, and for the most part proved successful. Ongoing investment in this area is vital.

The coalition this time relied on support from host nations – regional allies across the Gulf. This support is not guaranteed in future operations elsewhere, and the Navy in Operation Telic demonstrated its skill in being able to operate independently and flexibly, and to be largely self-sufficient at sea.

The men and women of the Navy and Marines showed adaptability, ingenuity and real grit in trying conditions. The medics had to work in atrociously unsanitary places, in the sheds and arsenals of Saddam's forces, and in the sand and mud of the desert. New ways of bringing medical help to the front line were discovered.

On the fighting front, the Marines, the helicopter flights, the Scimitars and Challenger 2s and the artillery combined in a true all-arms battle. Commanders and individuals acted on their own initiative – the essence of mission command.

The Navy showed itself to be a truly expeditionary force – one of the finest of the kind in the world. It could prepare and land a sizeable amphibious force in two months. With the Tomahawk cruise missiles it could strike targets at distance, with accuracy and surprise. The skills in minehunting and ordnance disposal are also world beaters – and at replenishment and support at sea, as the RFA like to say of themselves, "none does it better."

For the future there are prospects of more expeditionary missions, and for this new ships and equipment are about to join the fleet: the amphibious landing ships *HMS Albion* and *Bulwark*; the Type 45 destroyer; the new aircraft carriers and submarines. New radar, computer and communications systems will enhance the capability of the Navy to operate on its own or with the UK's coalition partners in what is known as 'network enabled capability'. This will be essential in pursuing campaigns against terrorism and other threats across the world.

Of course the older units and ships did sterling work. *HMS Roebuck* was due for a pension in March 2003, but now retirement has been deferred – so invaluable were the maps and data produced by her hydrographers.

The Royal Navy has a proud history and many aspects of this legacy are still pertinent – and were evident in Operation Telic. Nevertheless, the Royal Navy and its Marines do not stand still. They look to the future and to the conventional and unconventional threats that might confront them. But a fighting force is not just about equipment and procedures. The story of the Royal Navy and its Marines in Operation Telic is that of the men and women who make them what they are, were, and will continue to be.

IRAQ TIME LINES

From Mesopotamia to Iraq

BC
3500   Ur, the first city civilisation of history
630-562   Nebuchadnezzar rules the empire of Babylonia

AD
661   Murder of the founder of Shi'ism, Ali, 4th Imam and
                 son-in-law of Mohammed the Prophet
766 -809   rule of Harun al-Rashid, Caliph of Baghdad,
                 patron of the 1,001 Nights
1258   Baghdad sacked by the Mongols
1639   Baghdad captured by the Turks
1831   Ottomans retake Baghdad from Mamluks
1914   British take Basra
1916   General Townshend surrenders British forces at Kut
1917   British forces occupy Baghdad
1920   Britain given mandate over Iraq at San Remo conference
1921   King Faisal crowned in Baghdad
1927   First major oil finds near Kirkuk
1932   League of Nations ends British mandate and gives
                 Iraq independence
1941   Pro Nazi military coup by Rashid al-Kailani
                 British occupy Baghdad
1955   Baghdad Pact (beginning of Central Treaty Organization)
1956   Suez crisis, widespread riots in Iraq
1958   Coup by Brigadier Abd al-Karim Qasim,
                 monarchy overthrown and king assassinated
1963   Qasim assassinated by Baathists
                 Baathists ousted
1968   Baathists return to power

Iraq under Saddam

1979   Saddam Hussein sworn in as president
1980   Ayatollah al-Sadr and sister executed
                 40,000 Shiites expelled to Iran
                 (September) Iraq invades Iran
                 War with Iran begins (to 1988)
1982   Saddam Hussein asserts absolute power
1986   Iran captures Al Faw peninsula
1988   Campaign against Kurds. Villages round Halabja gassed
1990   (August) Iraq seizes Kuwait
1991   (March) Iraq expelled from Kuwait in Operation
                 Desert Storm/Desert Sabre
                 Peace talks at Al Safwan
                 (April) UN Security Council Resolution 687 demands
                 disarmament by Saddam

1995   Oil for Food agreement with UN
                 (UN Security Council Resolution 986)
1998   UN inspectors expelled by Saddam
                 UK and US four-day bombing campaign
                 ('Operation Desert Fox')
1999   UNMOVIC succeeds the UN inspection team
                 UNSCOM
2002   (November) UN Security Council passes resolution
                 1441 demanding immediate compliance with UN
                 disarmament requirements
                 (7 December) Iraq submits 12,000-page document
                 about arms
                 (19 December) chief UN Inspector Hans Blix says
                 report misses crucial details
2003   (11 January) Lead ships of British Naval Task Group
                 start to leave home waters

The Campaign

19-20 March   US air strike on Baghdad

20 March   attack by 3 Commando Brigade begins on Al Faw

21 March   CH-46 with Commando Brigade Reconnaissance
                   troop aboard crashes north of Kuwait

22 March   two Sea King helicopters of 849 Squadron crash
                   on patrol from *Ark Royal*

24 March   major operations in Al Faw by 40 Commando,
                   42 Commando breaks north for Umm Qasr
                   and Az Zubayr

28 March   *RFA Sir Galahad*, escorted by *HMS Sandown* and
                   HMS Roebuck, reaches Umm Qasr

30 March   Operation James: 40 Commando, elements of
                   42 Commando, and 845 Squadron helicopters in
                   major push into Basra from the south

6-8 April   Royal Marines and 7 Armoured Brigade take up
                   positions in Basra

9 April   US forces enter Baghdad

11 April   *Ark Royal* and other major units begin withdrawing

1 May   President Bush declares major combat phase of war
                   over from deck of carrier *USS Abraham Lincoln*

IN MEMORIAM

At around midnight GMT on 21 March, a US Marine Corps CH-46 Sea Knight helicopter crashed south of the Kuwait border with US and UK personnel aboard; there were no survivors. Eight personnel from 3 Commando Brigade died in the accident, along with four US aircrew:

* Colour Sergeant John Cecil, Royal Marines
* Lance Bombardier Llywelyn Karl Evans,
  29 Commando Regiment Royal Artillery
* Captain Philip Stuart Guy, Royal Marines
* Marine Sholto Hedenskog, Royal Marines
* Sergeant Les Hehir, 29 Commando Regiment Royal Artillery
* Operator Mechanic (Communications) Second Class Ian Seymour RN,
  148 Commando Battery Royal Artillery
* Warrant Officer Second Class Mark Stratford, Royal Marines
* Major Jason Ward, Royal Marines

At around 0130 GMT on 22 March, two Royal Navy Sea King Mk7 Airborne Early Warning helicopters collided over the Northern Arabian Gulf. There were no survivors from the six British and one US crew members aboard.

* Lieutenant Thomas Mullen Adams USN, 849 Naval Air Squadron
* Lieutenant Philip D. Green RN, 849 Naval Air Squadron
* Lieutenant Antony King RN, 849 Naval Air Squadron
* Lieutenant Marc A. Lawrence RN, 849 Naval Air Squadron
* Lieutenant Philip West RN, 849 Naval Air Squadron
* Lieutenant James Williams RN, 849 Naval Air Squadron
* Lieutenant Andrew S. Wilson RN, 849 Naval Air Squadron

On 30 March, a Royal Marine officer died of natural causes:

* Major Steve Ballard, 3 Commando Brigade Royal Marines

A Royal Marine was killed in action during fighting on 30 March:

* Marine Christopher R. Maddison,
  9 Assault Squadron Royal Marines

Main Royal Navy, Royal Marines and Royal Fleet Auxiliary units deployed in Operation Telic

HMS Ark Royal	Aircraft carrier /in helicopter carrier role
HMS Ocean	Helicopter carrier
HMS Chatham	Type 22 frigate
HMS Marlborough	Type 23 frigate
HMS Richmond	Type 23 frigate
HMS Edinburgh	Type 42 destroyer
HMS Liverpool	Type 42 destroyer
HMS York	Type 42 destroyer
RFA Sir Galahad	Landing ship logistic
RFA Sir Tristram	Landing ship logistic
RFA Sir Percivale	Landing ship logistic
HMS Turbulent	Trafalgar class nuclear powered attack submarine
HMS Splendid	Swiftsure class nuclear powered attack submarine
RFA Sir Bedivere	Mine Counter Measures Vessel Support Ship
HMS Bangor	Sandown class Mine Counter Measures Vessel
HMS Blyth	Sandown class Mine Counter Measures Vessel
HMS Sandown	Sandown class Mine Counter Measures Vessel
HMS Brocklesby	Hunt class Mine Counter Measures Vessel
HMS Grimsby	Sandown class Mine Counter Measures Vessel
HMS Ramsey	Sandown class Mine Counter Measures Vessel
HMS Shoreham	Sandown class Mine Counter Measures Vessel
HMS Ledbury	Hunt class Mine Counter Measures Vessel
HMS Roebuck	Hydrographic survey vessel
RFA Bayleaf	Fleet support tanker
RFA Orangeleaf	Fleet support tanker
RFA Brambleleaf	Fleet support tanker
RFA Grey Rover	Small fleet tanker
RFA Fort Rosalie	Fleet support stores ship
RFA Fort Austin	Fleet support stores ship
RFA Fort Victoria	Fleet support tanker and stores ship
RFA Diligence	Forward repair ship
RFA Argus	Primary casualty receiving ship
RFA Sea Crusader	Strategic lift ro-ro

Naval Air Squadrons
814 Naval Air Squadron
815 Naval Air Squadron
820 Naval Air Squadron
845 Naval Air Squadron
847 Naval Air Squadron
849 Naval Air Squadron

Royal Naval Reservists from:
HMS Cambria, HMS Calliope, HMS Caroline, HMS Dalriada, HMS Eaglet, HMS Flying Fox, HMS Forward, HMS King Alfred, HMS President, HMS Scotia, HMS Sherwood, HMS Vivi, HMS Wildfire, RNR branch at HMS Heron

Royal Marines and Commando Forces
HQ 3 Commando Brigade
40 Commando
42 Commando
UK Landing Force Command Support Group
Commando Logistic Regiment Royal Marines
29 Commando Regiment Royal Artillery
539 Assault Squadron Royal Marines
9 Assault Squadron Royal Marines
59 Independent Commando Squadron Royal Engineers
131 Independent Commando Squadron Royal Engineers (Volunteers)

Plus elements of:
45 Commando
HQ Commander UK Amphibious Forces
20 Commando Battery RA
Fleet Protection Group Royal Marines
4 Assault Squadron Royal Marines
Royal Marines Band Service
Royal Marines Reserve City of London, Scotland, Bristol, Merseyside, Tyne

Attachments
C Squadron the Queen's Dragoon Guards
C Squadron the Royal Scots Dragoon Guards
18 Squadron RAF

Author's Note
I would like to thank all the men and women from all arms of the Royal Navy who agreed to meet me, give interviews, and share notes and photographs in the preparation of this text. The mistakes, of course, are mine. It was a pleasure and a privilege to meet you all, too many to mention by name. It is your book.
Robert Fox